Human Body

Easy Make & Learn Projects

BY DONALD M. SILVER AND PATRICIA J. WYNNE

SCHOLASTIC
PROFESSIONAL BOOKS

NEW YORK • TORONTO • LONDON • AUCKLAND • SYDNEY
MEXICO CITY • NEW DELHI • HONG KONG

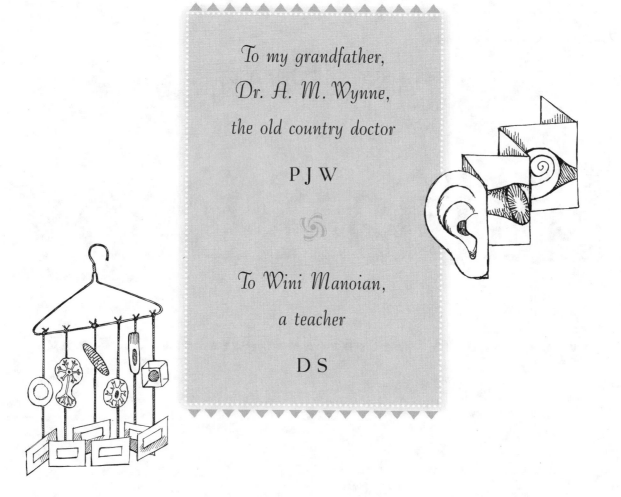

To my grandfather,
Dr. A. M. Wynne,
the old country doctor

P J W

To Wini Manoian,
a teacher

D S

Front cover and interior design by Kathy Massaro
Cover and interior artwork by Patricia J. Wynne

ISBN: 0-439-04087-6
Copyright © 1999 by Donald M. Silver and Patricia J. Wynne
All rights reserved.
Printed in the U.S.A.

Contents

Introduction

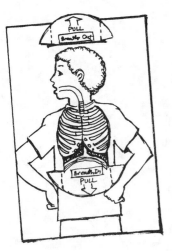

Welcome to *Easy Make & Learn Projects: Human Body*! The human body is a great science topic to explore with elementary students. Children are naturally curious about their bodies and have lots of firsthand knowledge and experience about how their own bodies function. They know they are growing, losing teeth, and changing, and they want to know why!

The models, manipulatives, accompanying background information, and lessons in this book will help motivate and teach your students about the human body. Students will learn what these body parts look like, what they do, and where they are located. Many models contain text and labels that will increase students' science vocabulary and improve their reading skills.

Many of the concepts presented in this book meet a number of

National Science Education Content Standards for Life Science (Grades K–4)

The Characteristics of Organisms

◎ Organisms, including humans, have basic needs, like air, water, and food.

◎ All organisms have specific structures that serve different functions in growth, survival, and reproduction. Humans have specialized body structures for walking, thinking, seeing, and talking, for example.

◎ The behavior of individual organisms is influenced by internal cues, like hunger or pain, and by external cues, like sounds, smells, or changes in temperature. Humans, as well as other organisms, have senses that help them detect these cues.

the National Science Education Standards, the criteria intended to guide the quality of science teaching and learning in this country. The standards support a hands-on, inquiry-based approach to learning. The chart on page 4 shows how the topics in this book correlate with the Life Science Content Standards for students in kindergarten through grade four.

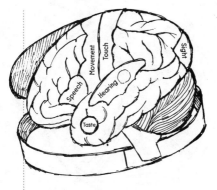

What's Inside

The models and manipulatives in this book allow you and your students to investigate the human body's structures and functions. The models in each chapter focus on a particular system of the body. The chapters are independent and can be used in any order. Featured within each chapter are the following sections:

Model Illustration
This picture, labeled with the model's name, shows how the finished model looks. It can be helpful to use as a reference when making the model.

Body Basics
Background information on the chapter's topic and concepts is contained here. Use some or all of this information with the Teaching With the Model section, depending on the level of your students.

Making the Model
These are easy-to-follow instructions with diagrams for assembling the models. See the helpful hints for following the instructions on the next page.

Teaching With the Model
This section provides a step-by-step lesson map with discussion questions for using the models to teach the chapter's main concepts.

Explore More!
In this section you'll find related activities to extend your students' investigation of the topic.

Helpful Hints for Model-Making

◎ The thickest black lines on the reproducible pages are CUT lines.

◎ Dotted lines on the reproducible pages are FOLD lines.

◎ Some models have slits or windows to cut out. An easy way to make them is to fold the paper at a right angle to the solid cut lines. Then snip along the lines from the crease of the fold inward.

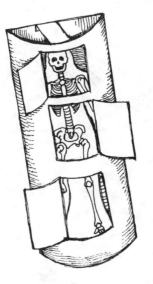

◎ Often glue sticks can be substituted for tape. However, some situations, for example, creating flaps, require tape.

◎ If students will be coloring the models and using tape, have them color first so they won't have to color over the tape.

◎ Some models are more challenging to assemble than others. Read through each Making the Model section (or make the model yourself) beforehand to determine if it's appropriate for your students to do on their own. You can choose to make a more challenging model yourself and use it as a classroom demonstration tool.

◎ If a single model will be handled a great deal, consider creating it from heavier paper. Simply paste the reproducible page onto construction paper before beginning assembly.

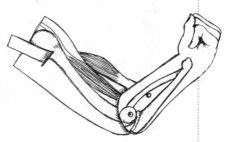

The Body Book

Students make a book about the human body that introduces them to a number of systems and organs in the body.

The Body Book

Body Basics

The human body is a complex living organism that takes in food and air to provide itself with nutrients and energy for moving and thinking. The body accomplishes these tasks thanks to living organs and tissues as well as nonliving parts, such as water, vitamins, and minerals.

An *organ* is a group of tissues that perform a specific function. For example, the heart pumps blood. In turn, *tissues* are groups of similar specialized cells—the smallest living parts in the body. The organs and tissues of the body are divided into organ *systems* based on the function they accomplish. Seven organ systems are featured in this book.

- The *integumentary system* is the skin, hair, and nails. It protects the body.

- The *skeletal system's* bones, cartilage, and joints provide a moving framework for the body.

- The muscles of the *muscular system* produce movement and generate heat in the body.

- The brain, spinal cord, and nerves make up the *nervous system*, which takes in information, allows communication within the body, and controls body functions.

- The *circulatory system* is the heart and blood vessels that pump and transport blood throughout the body.

- The lungs and other breathing organs make up the *respiratory system*. They work to exchange oxygen for carbon dioxide in the blood.

- The stomach, liver, intestines, gallbladder, and esophagus are all food-processing organs of the *digestive system*. They work to break down food and absorb its nutrients.

Materials

- reproducible pages 9 and 10
- scissors
- crayons, colored pencils, or markers (optional)

Making the Model

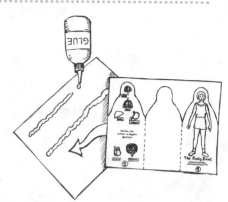

1 Photocopy pages 9 and 10 as double-sided copies or glue the pages back to back. The heads of the figure on both sides should be at the top of the page.

2 Cut along the solid black line at the top of the page.

3 Fold back and forth along the dotted lines so that page 1 is on top and page 5 is underneath.

4 Color the books if desired.

Teaching With the Model

1 What is the human body made of? (living tissues, cells, organs, and nonliving chemicals, like water, vitamins, and minerals) Ask students what a cell is (smallest living part of the body), what tissue is (groups of cells with a particular task or specialization), and what an organ is (groups of tissues that perform a specific function). Challenge students first to name an organ and then identify the tissue and cells that it is made of. (For example, the brain is made up of brain tissue, which is made up of nerve cells.)

2 What are some things the human body can do? (eat, move, feel, see, think, remember, and so on.)

3 Which systems of the human body are featured in THE BODY BOOK? (skeletal system and muscular system) Challenge students to name the human body system that each of the organs on page 5 belongs to. (brain—nervous system; lungs—respiratory system; liver, stomach, and intestines—digestive system; heart—circulatory system) Have students compare and contrast the functions and organs of these systems.

The Body Book

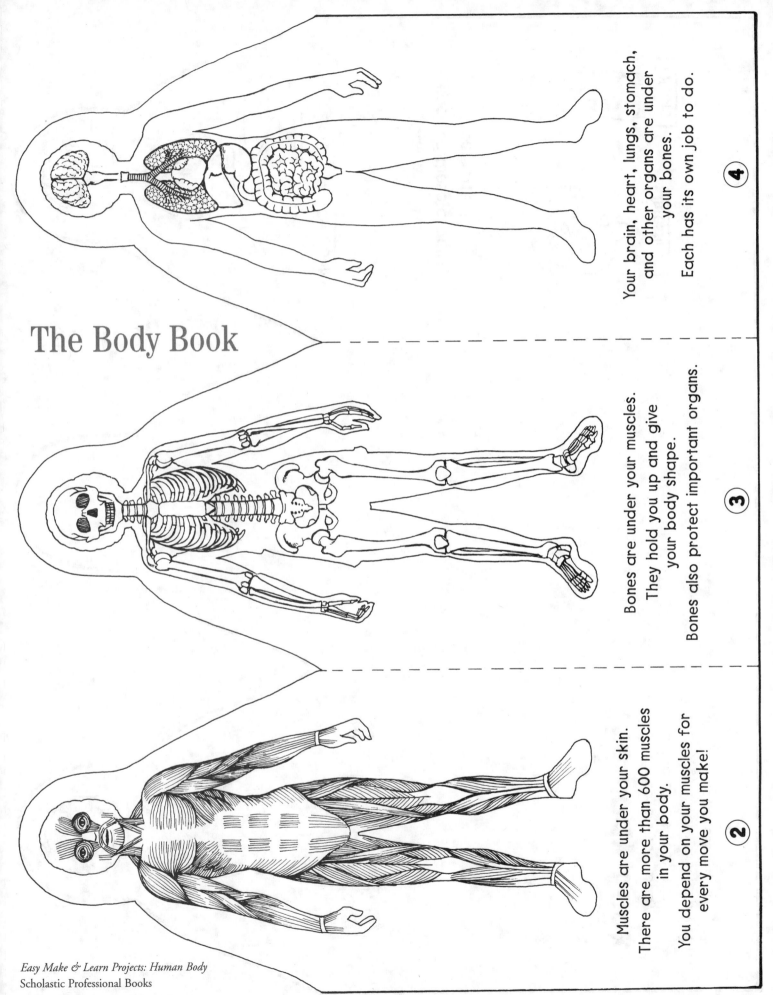

Muscles are under your skin.
There are more than 600 muscles in your body.
You depend on your muscles for every move you make!

(2)

Bones are under your muscles.
They hold you up and give your body shape.
Bones also protect important organs.

(3)

Your brain, heart, lungs, stomach, and other organs are under your bones.
Each has its own job to do.

(4)

Easy Make & Learn Projects: Human Body
Scholastic Professional Books

The Body Book

Brain

Lungs

Liver

Stomach

Can you find each of these organs on page 4?

Heart

Intestines

⑤

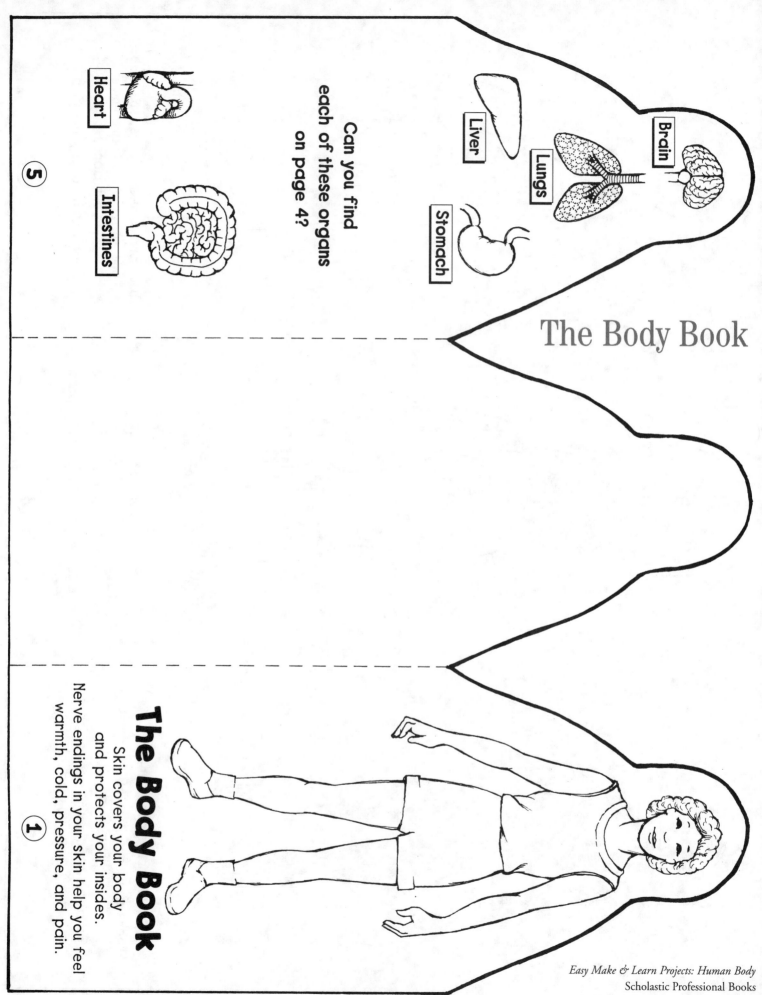

The Body Book

Skin covers your body and protects your insides. Nerve endings in your skin help you feel warmth, cold, pressure, and pain.

①

Cell Mobile

This mobile illustrates six kinds
of body cells.

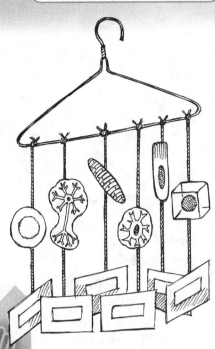

Body Basics

Cells are the smallest living (or organic) parts of the human body. Nearly all body cells are too tiny to be seen without a microscope. All cells grow and use energy to stay alive. Cells have different sizes, shapes, and jobs. Heart muscle tissue is made up of special kinds of muscle cells, for example. Eye cells detect light; lung cells exchange gases; and stomach cells break down food.

The model features the following six kinds of cells.

◎ *Nerve cells* have long rootlike ends that connect to other neurons in chains that shuttle information around the body.

◎ *Bone cells* contain the mineral calcium, which gives bone its strength.

◎ *Red blood cells* are the most numerous cells in the body. Their unique caved-in shape helps them travel through blood vessels and deliver oxygen to all body cells.

◎ *Skin cells* are like building blocks that create a protective layer that covers the body.

◎ *Intestinal cells* end in many fingerlike villi through which the body absorbs digested nutrients.

◎ *Skeletal muscle cells* make up the bundles of muscle fibers that power the voluntary muscles. The striations, or bands, in these cells help them contract and pull on the bones to which they are attached. This allows the bones to move.

Materials

- reproducible page 13
- scissors
- tape
- wire hanger
- 6 pieces of string of varying lengths
- 6 sheets of different colored paper, each about 2 by 3 inches
- crayons, colored pencils, or markers (optional)

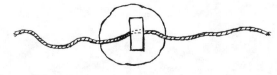

Making the Model

1 Photocopy page 13. Color the cells if desired.

2 Cut out all 12 pieces along the solid black lines.

3 Turn a cell over. Place one piece of string on the back of the cell so the cell is about halfway down the length of the string. Tape the string to the back of the cell as shown.

4 Repeat step 3 for the 5 remaining cells.

5 Cut the pieces of colored paper into different shapes, such as circles, squares, and triangles, if desired. (Make sure that they are large enough for a label.) Tape a label to each piece of colored paper.

6 Match each cell to its label using the numbers. Tape the correct label to the bottom of the string with its cell.

7 Tie the free end of each string to the coat hanger. (See the finished model drawing on page 11.)

Teaching With the Model

1 Have students look at the different cells of the CELL MOBILE. Discuss some of the characteristics of each kind of cell.

2 What is a cell? (a building block of tissue) Are cells alive? (yes)

3 Are all cells the same? (no) Why not? (Each kind has a different task and has a special feature for doing that job.)

4 Ask students to describe the shape and characteristics of each kind of cell in the model. Challenge them to think and theorize about how the cell's shape and characteristics help it perform its job.

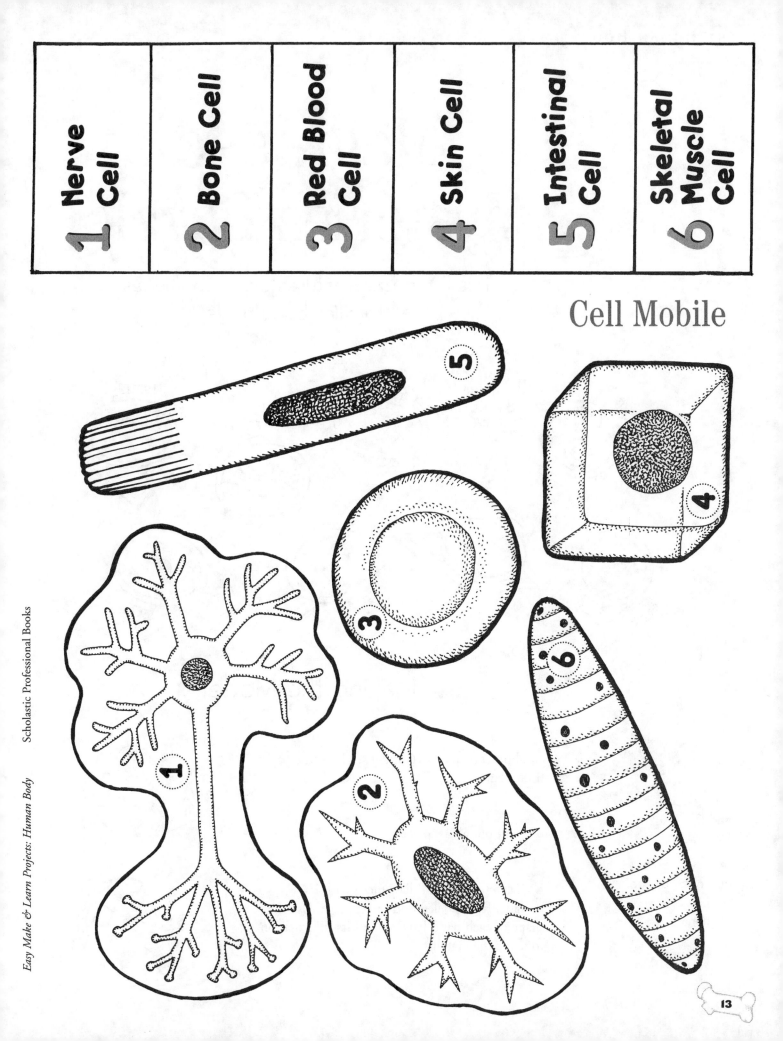

Cell Mobile

1 Nerve Cell	2 Bone Cell	3 Red Blood Cell	4 Skin Cell	5 Intestinal Cell	6 Skeletal Muscle Cell

Easy Make & Learn Projects: Human Body   Scholastic Professional Books

13

Magnified Mysteries Puzzle

This fun puzzle features close-up images of familiar body parts.

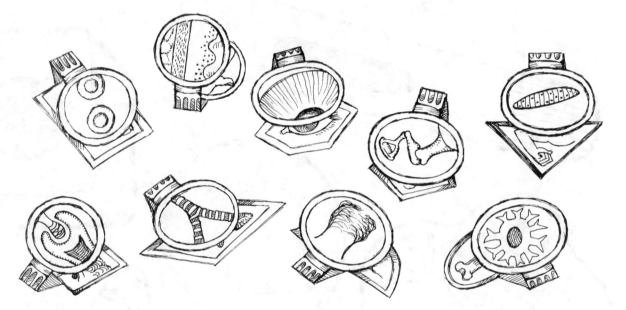

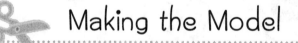

Making the Model

1 Photocopy pages 16 and 17. Color the pages if desired.

2 Cut out all 18 pieces.

3 Match each hand lens piece with its unmagnified, labeled body-part piece. Use the shape of each hand lens tag and its information to make the match.

Materials

◎ reproducible pages 16 and 17
◎ scissors
◎ tape
◎ crayons, colored pencils, or markers (optional)

4 Turn over a hand lens piece and tape its matched piece over its like-shaped tag, as shown.

5 Repeat step 4 for the remaining eight hand lens pieces. Turn the nine joined pieces over and fold each along its dotted line. The unmagnified body part is revealed when the round lens of the hand lens is lifted.

Teaching With the Model

1 Use the MAGNIFIED MYSTERIES PUZZLE to spark student interest in learning about the human body. As you complete each chapter in this book, challenge students to label each puzzle piece with the organ system it is part of. (They can label the ear and eye pieces "senses.")

2 Use the puzzle again at the end of the unit to reinforce and review what students have learned. Consider making a second set of the pieces without the handles and tags for students to match just by recognizing images.

Explore More!

Time Line: My Body

Help students appreciate their own bodies. Invite them to create personal time lines, noting dates and events of importance. Have them start with the day of their birth, noting their weights and lengths. Then have students note their heights over the years as well as other "body events" of importance, like "learned to walk," "started talking," "broke a bone," "got glasses," and so on. Encourage students to illustrate their time lines with old photographs or drawings.

Magnified Mysteries Puzzle

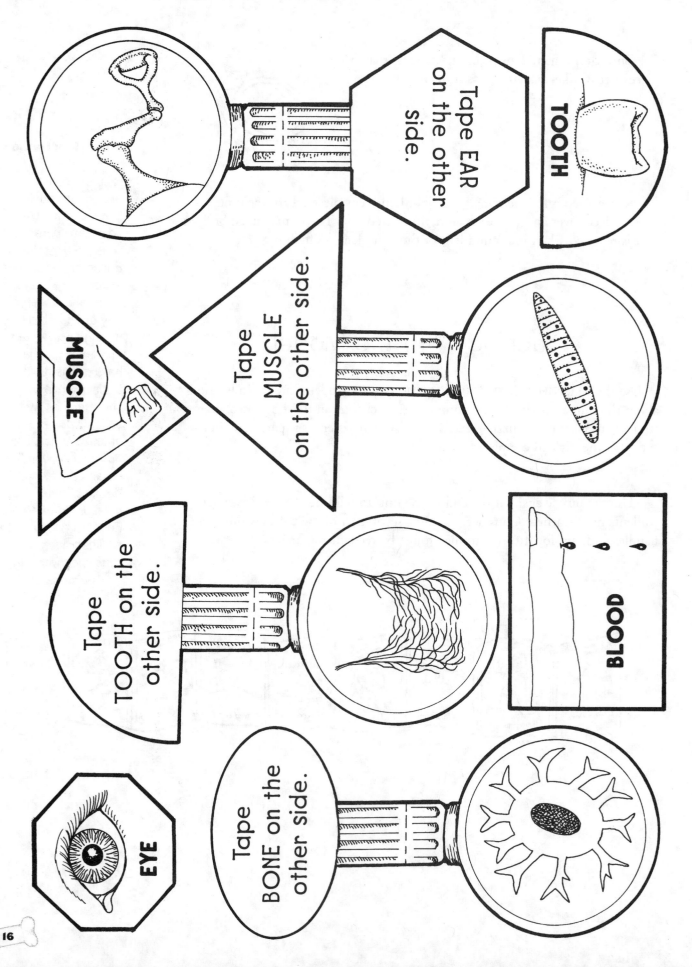

Tape EAR on the other side.

TOOTH

Tape MUSCLE on the other side.

MUSCLE

Tape TOOTH on the other side.

BLOOD

Tape BONE on the other side.

EYE

Magnified Mysteries Puzzle

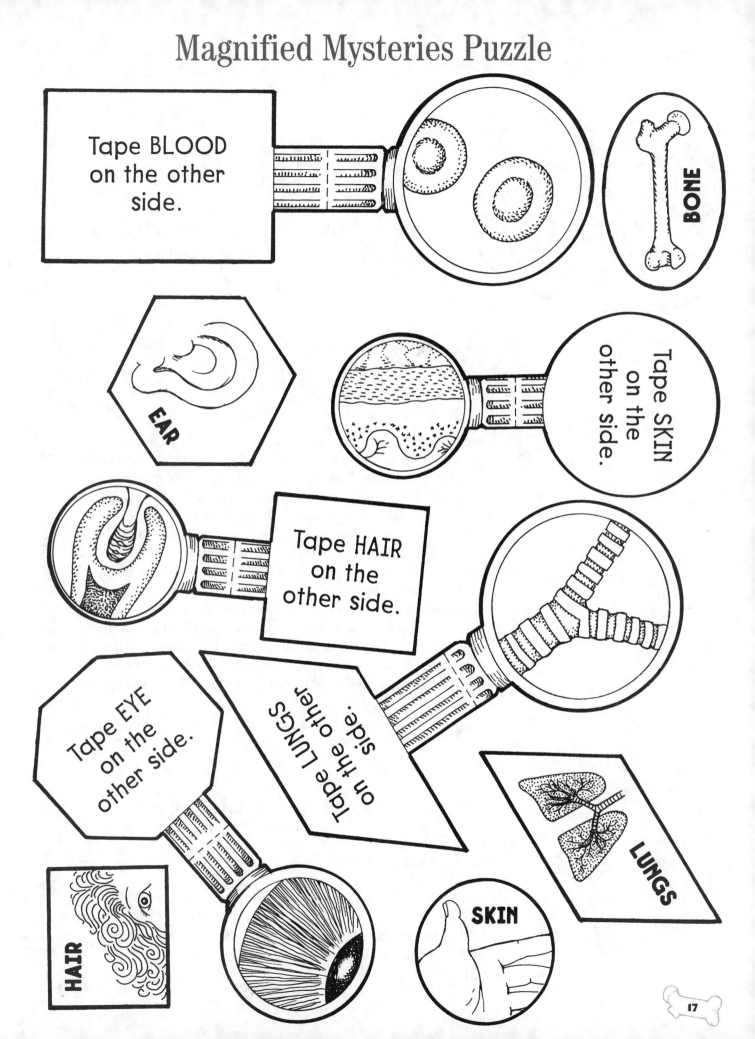

Tape BLOOD on the other side.

BONE

EAR

Tape SKIN on the other side.

Tape HAIR on the other side.

Tape EYE on the other side.

Tape LUNGS on the other side.

LUNGS

HAIR

SKIN

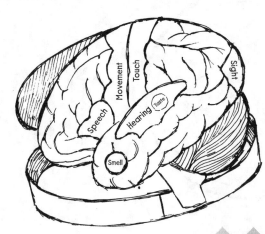

Brain Hat

This hat illustrates important parts and control centers of the brain.

Body Basics

The *nervous system* is made up of the brain, spinal cord, and nerves. Its task is to gather information from inside and outside the body, transmit messages, and activate muscle movement. The brain is the coordinating command center of the nervous system. It continually receives information through the sense organs, processes that information, and sends out messages that control body functions and actions. The brain has three major divisions—the *cerebrum, cerebellum,* and *brain stem*. The cerebrum is the largest. It includes the two hemispheres and 85 percent of the brain overall. The cerebrum is where most of the brain's higher functions, like speaking, hearing, and thinking, occur. The cerebellum coordinates body movement and balance. It's located at the lower back of the brain. The brain stem connects the cerebellum to the spinal cord and is responsible for the body's most basic functions, like breathing and blood pressure.

Materials

- reproducible pages 20 and 21
- scissors
- tape
- crayons, colored pencils, or markers (optional)

Making the Model

1 Photocopy pages 20 and 21. Color the pages if desired.

2 Cut out the pieces along the solid black lines.

3 Fold the brain piece along the dotted line between the left and right sides. Fold the wide strip along its dotted line.

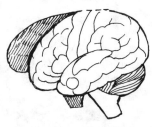

4 Tape together the two long, narrow strips to make a headband, as shown. Students with larger heads can add in the HEADBAND STRETCHER piece.

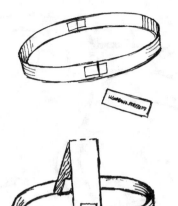

5 Tape each end of the wide strip to the headband, as shown.

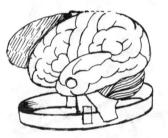

6 Open the brain piece and rest it on top of the wide strip so that both folded creases overlap. Tape the brain piece to the wide band.

7 Match the words and shapes of the control center pieces (speech, touch, and so on) to their places on the left side of the brain. Use rolled-up pieces of tape to attach them to the brain hat. (See the finished model drawing on page 18.)

Teaching With the Model

1 What parts of the body make up the nervous system? (brain, spinal cord, and nerves) What does the nervous system do? (gathers information from inside and outside the body, transmits messages, and activates muscle movement)

2 What is the brain's function? (coordinates the tasks of the nervous system) What is it made of? (billions of nerve cells, or neurons) Where is it located? (inside the protective skull bones)

3 Ask students the function of the cerebrum (higher functions, like speaking, hearing, and thinking), the cerebellum (coordination of body movements and balance), and the brain stem. (basic body functions like breathing and blood pressure) Have partners put on their BRAIN HATS and, looking at each other's hat, pick out these three parts labeled on the right side of the hat.

Brain Hat

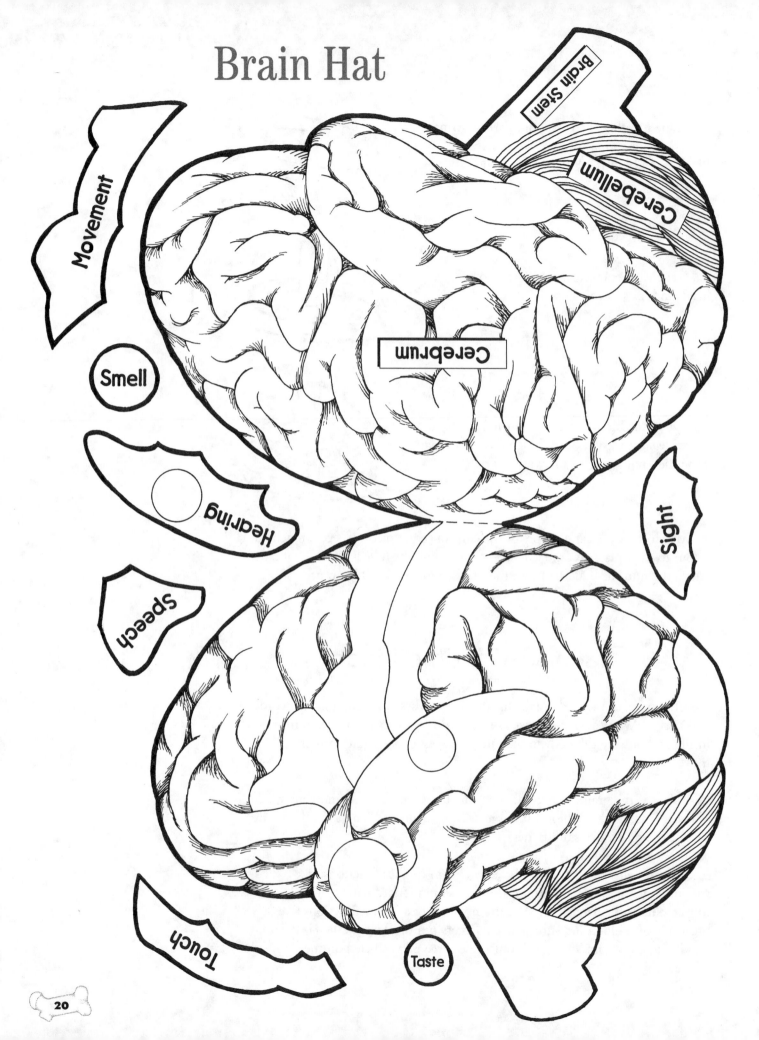

Movement

Brain Stem

Cerebellum

Cerebrum

Smell

Hearing

Sight

Speech

Touch

Taste

Brain Hat

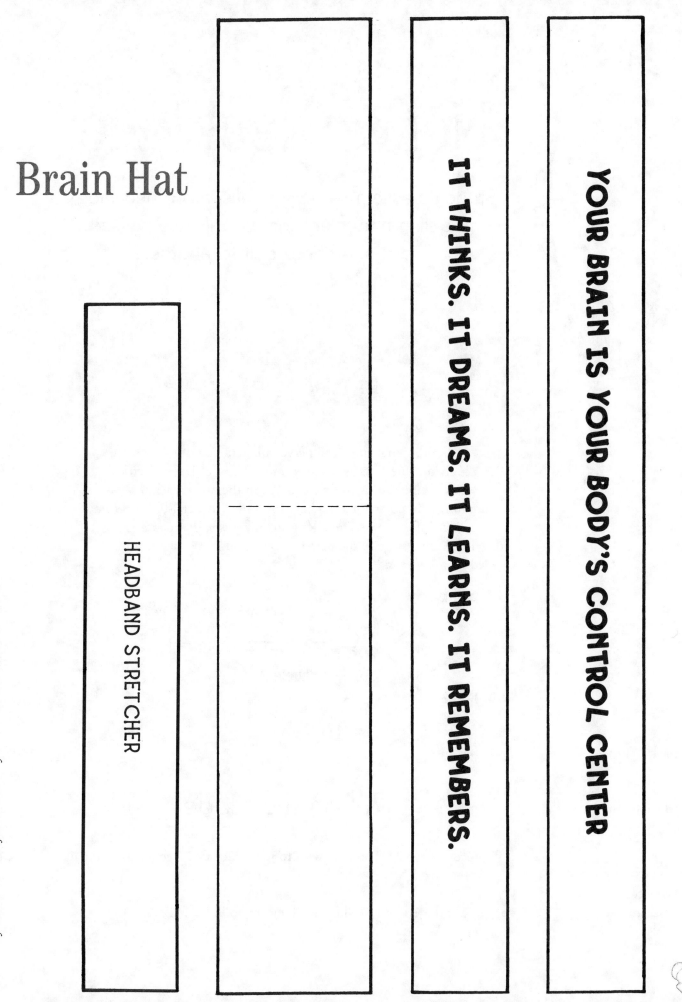

HEADBAND STRETCHER

IT THINKS. IT DREAMS. IT LEARNS. IT REMEMBERS.

YOUR BRAIN IS YOUR BODY'S CONTROL CENTER

Nerve Necklace

Students assemble nerve cells into a necklace, modeling how electrical signals are passed from one nerve cell to another

Body Basics

The brain, spinal cord, and nerves are made up of billions of individual nerve cells called *neurons*. These cells fire electrical nerve impulses fueled by chemicals in the body. Each neuron has a roundish cell body with a *nucleus* surrounded by petal-like *dendrites* that receive information, and a long stemlike *axon* that passes along the electrical message to the next neuron through rootlike tendrils called *terminal ends*.

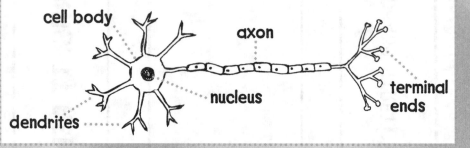

cell body

axon

nucleus

dendrites

terminal ends

Materials

- reproducible page 24
- scissors
- tape
- 24-inch piece of string
- crayons, colored pencils, or markers (optional)

Making the Model

1 Photocopy page 24. You may wish to reproduce the page on colored paper or color the boxes.

2 Cut out the 16 nerve cell boxes along the solid black lines.

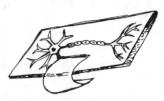

3 Fold each box lengthwise along its dotted line.

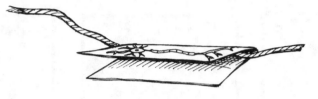

4 Thread the string through each folded piece and tape closed, as shown. Be sure the boxes line up opposite end to opposite end.

5 Tie the ends of the string together for a necklace. (Note: You can also make belts using more boxes and a longer piece of string.)

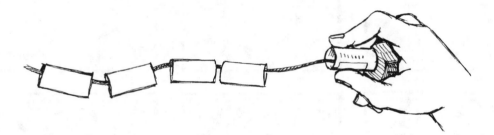

Teaching With the Model

1 Invite students to wear their NERVE NECKLACES. Have students look at one of the necklace's neurons and discuss what a neuron is and what it does. (nerve cell, passes signals along nerves) Ask: Where are neurons found? (nerves, brain, spinal cord)

2 Ask students to describe the neurons on their necklaces. Point out the cell body, axon ends, and dendrites of the cells. Invite students to label these parts on several of their necklace neurons.

3 How are neurons arranged inside nerves or brain tissue? (in chains and webs with the axon of one neuron next to the dendrites of another)

Explore More!

Chain Reaction

Students can pretend to be a chain of neurons and transmit a signal. Have students stand in a circle and hold hands. A Starter student squeezes his or her right hand. As soon as the person next to the Starter feels the squeeze, he or she passes along the squeeze to the right. It goes around the circle until the squeeze makes it back to the Starter's left hand, and he or she says, "Stop!" Time how long it takes the signal to make it around the circle going to the left and to the right. Does the time shorten with practice?

Easy Make & Learn Projects: Human Body

Scholastic Professional Books

Sliding Eye (*Sight*)

This model illustrates the inner and outer structures of the eye.

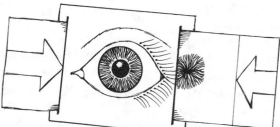

Body Basics

Every day the human body takes in light, sound waves, odor and taste molecules, and pressure and temperature information from the skin and translates all of it into images, sounds, smells, tastes, and sensations that allow us to experience our environment. Our five senses are our link to the outside world.

How do we see? Light reflected off objects enters the eye through the hole in the *iris* called the *pupil*. It then travels through and is focused by the *lens* onto the *retina* at the back of the eye. Millions of light-sensitive nerve cells cover the retina. These nerve cells react to the light and send an upside-down image to the brain. The brain then puts the image right side up and processes it, figuring out what is "sees."

Making the Model

1 Photocopy page 27. Color the page if desired.

2 Cut the sheet in half along the horizontal solid black line.

Materials

◎ reproducible page 27
◎ scissors
◎ tape
◎ crayons, colored pencils, or markers (optional)

Look Into My Eyes

Have partners look at each other's pupils. Turn off the lights for a few minutes, then turn them back on. As soon as the lights go on, have each pair check the size of their pupils. Are they bigger or smaller? (bigger) What happens after a few minutes? (pupils shrink)

3 Cut out the hatch-lined center of the eye on the bottom piece. Also cut open the two slits on both sides of the eye.

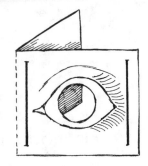

4 Fold the eye piece in half along the dotted line so that the eye is on top. Tape the right edges together, as shown.

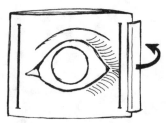

5 Thread the sliding piece through so the images appear inside the cut-out eye.

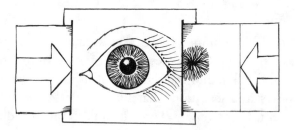

Teaching With the Model

1 Ask students to look at each other's eyes. What parts can they see? (iris, pupil) If a doctor looked into your eyes with a light, what might he or she see? (blood vessels, lens, retina)

2 Have students compare the inside and outside of the eye by sliding the long strip of their model back and forth. Matching arrow 1 with the left side of the eye shows the outer structures of the eye. Matching arrow 2 with the right side shows the inner structures.

3 Challenge students to use the model to explain how their eyes allow them to see. Also discuss ways students can take care of their eyes (never look directly at the sun, go to the eye doctor for regular check-ups, wear glasses, if needed)

Sliding Eye

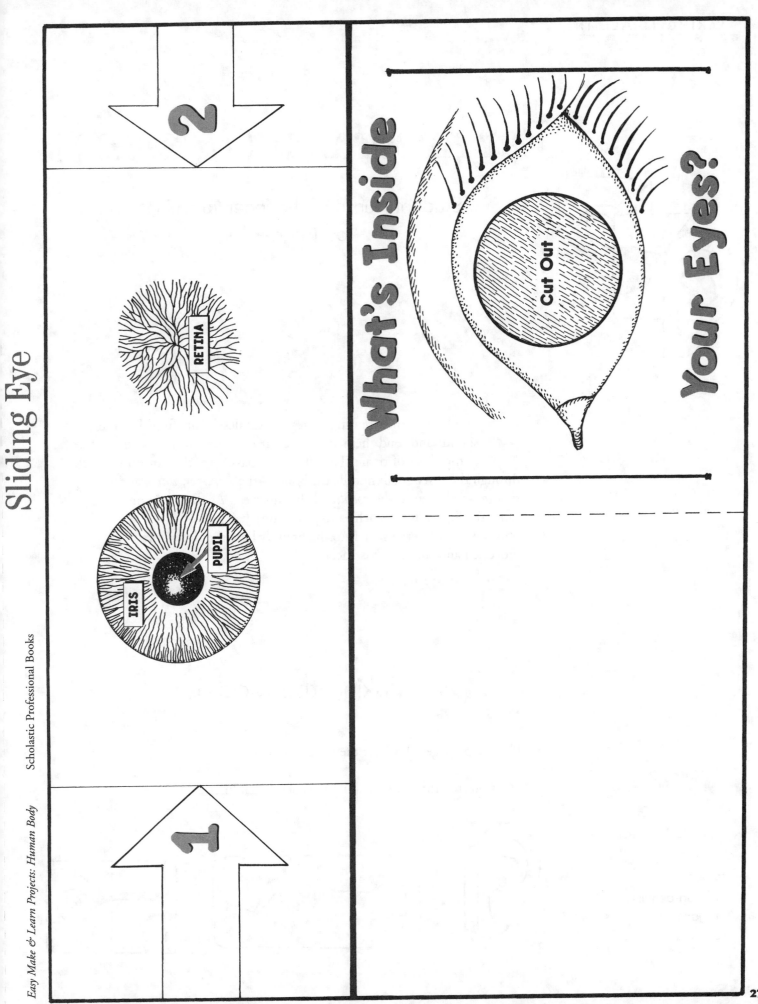

RETINA

IRIS
PUPIL

2

1

What's Inside

Cut Out

Your Eyes?

Ear Accordion (*Hearing*)

Students "unfold" the inner workings of the ear.

Body Basics

S ound travels in vibrating waves. Outer fleshy ears funnel in the sounds and send them along the *ear canal* toward the *eardrum*, a thin sheet of tissue. The vibrations pass from the eardrum through the three small middle ear bones—the *hammer, anvil,* and *stirrup*—and then to the *cochlea* of the inner ear. As the vibrations cause the liquid in the cochlea to move, tiny hairs set off the transmission of nerve signals to the brain, where the signals are processed and the sound is "heard."

Making the Model

1 Photocopy page 30. Color the page if desired.

2 Cut out the three pieces along the solid black lines.

Materials

- reproducible page 30
- scissors
- tape or glue
- colored pencils, crayons, or markers (optional)

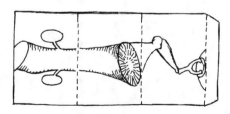

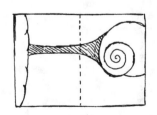

3 Tape or glue the three pieces together to make one long strip, as shown.

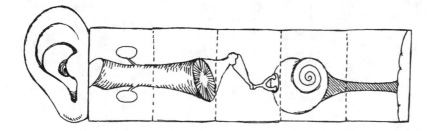

4 Fold the strip accordion style along the dotted lines so that the outer ear is on top.

Teaching With the Model

Ask students to open and read their EAR ACCORDION models. Check for understanding by asking the following questions:

- What parts are in the outer ear? (part on the outside of the head, ear canal, eardrum) What is its job? (gather sound waves and funnel them into the ear canal until they reach the eardrum and make it vibrate)

- What parts make up the middle ear? (the small hammer, anvil, and stirrup bones) What is their job? (pass along the vibrations from the eardrum)

- What makes up the inner ear? (cochlea and hearing nerves) What is their job? (translate the vibrations into nerve signals that are sent to the brain)

Hear, Hear!

Let students make a model of the ear canal and eardrum to investigate how vibrations produce sound. Divide the class into pairs and provide each with an empty bathroom tissue tube, a four-inch square of waxed paper, and a small rubber band. Show them how to fasten the waxed paper over one end of the tube with a rubber band, pulling it taut. Have one student place a finger lightly against the waxed paper "eardrum" while his or her partner speaks into the other end of the tube. What happens? (The student touching the eardrum will feel a tickle as the eardrum moves back and forth very quickly, or vibrates. This is how sound vibrations travel into the inner ear.)

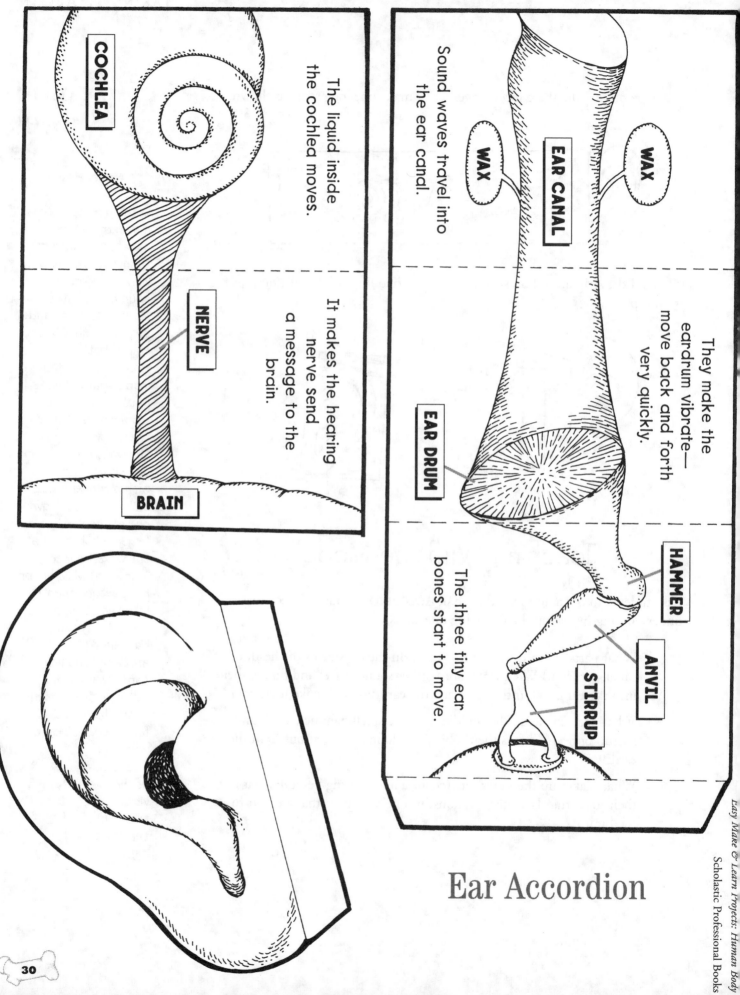

COCHLEA

The liquid inside the cochlea moves.

NERVE

It makes the hearing nerve send a message to the brain.

BRAIN

Sound waves travel into the ear canal.

WAX

EAR CANAL

WAX

They make the eardrum vibrate— move back and forth very quickly.

EAR DRUM

HAMMER

ANVIL

STIRRUP

The three tiny ear bones start to move.

Ear Accordion

Easy Make & Learn Projects: Human Body
Scholastic Professional Books

Want a Taste? (*Taste*)

Students construct a model of the tongue and mouth to get a close-up look at their taste buds.

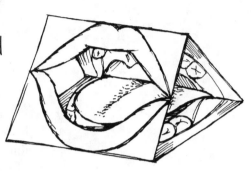

Body Basics

The tongue's surface is covered with about 10,000 *taste buds*, the sensory organs for taste. Each taste bud has an opening through which saliva enters, carrying dissolved food molecules that are then identified by the taste buds as either salty, sour, bitter, or sweet. Nerve endings then send information to the brain about the foods being eaten.

Making the Model

1 Photocopy page 33. Color the page if desired.

2 Cut out the three pieces along the solid black lines.

3 Cut open the slot at the back of the mouth. Then fold the piece over along the dotted lines.

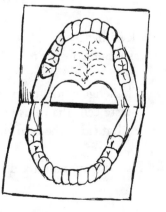

Materials

- reproducible page 33
- scissors
- tape
- colored pencils, crayons, or markers (optional)

4 Insert the flap at the back of the tongue piece into the mouth slot as shown.

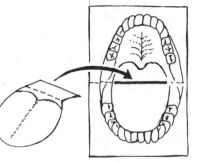

5 Fold the tongue tab back down along the dotted line and tape it to the back of the mouth piece.

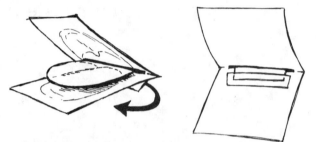

6 Cut out the hatch-lined area of the lips piece. Tape the top of the lips piece to the top of the other piece and its bottom to the bottom of the lips piece.

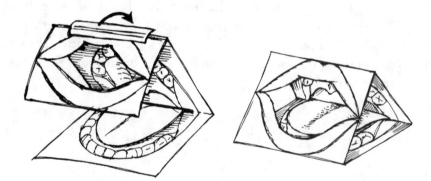

Teaching With the Model

1 Ask students to look at their models. Have them identify the tongue and the taste buds on the model.

2 Challenge students to explain how taste buds taste. (Taste buds are made up of taste cells that sense the chemicals in food and send taste signals to nerves that carry them to the brain.)

3 How many main food tastes are there? (four—sweet, sour, salty, bitter)

Want a Taste?

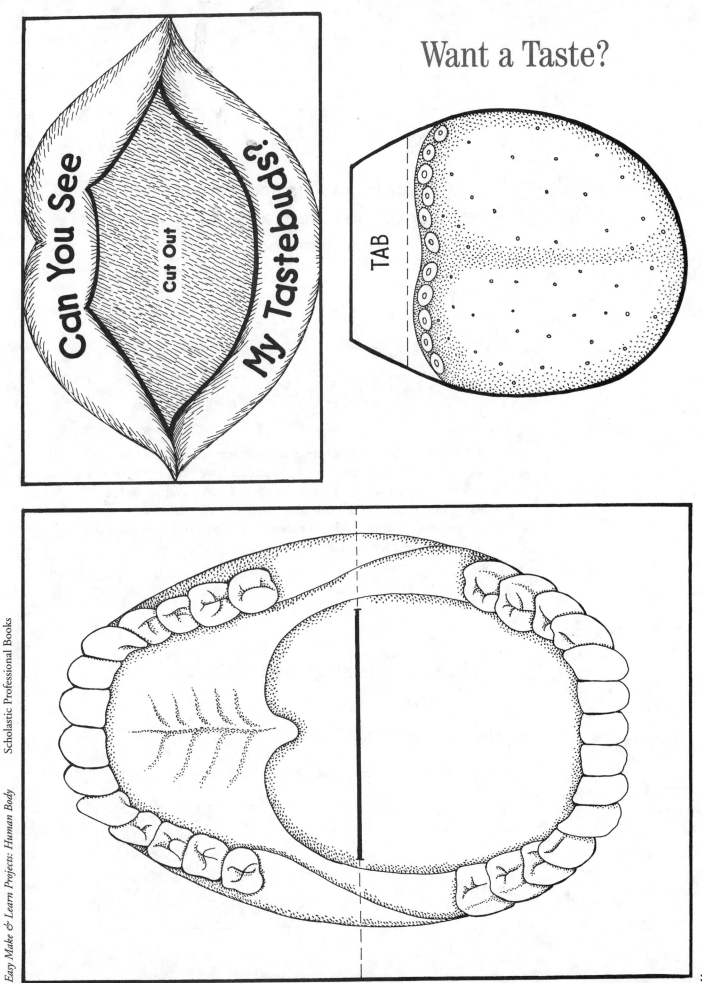

Can You See My Tastebuds?

Cut Out

TAB

Take a Whiff (*Smell*)

Students make a lift-the-flap mini-poster to discover how their sense of smell works and what odors are.

Body Basics

As we breathe, our noses take in air that carries odors. Odors are actually invisible molecules of gas that have been released by a substance. The odors enter the nostrils and travel up to the *olfactory bulb* at the top of both *nasal cavities*. Here the odors stimulate nerve cells that relay messages to the part of the brain that identifies different kinds of smells.

Making the Model

Materials

- reproducible page 36
- scissors
- tape
- colored pencils, crayons, or markers (optional)

1 Photocopy page 36. Color the page if desired.

2 Cut out the four pieces along the solid black lines.

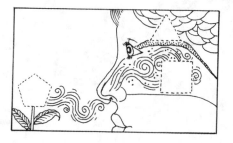

3 Tape each small piece where it belongs on the same-shaped dotted outline on the large piece, as shown. The tape is like a hinge so each piece can be easily lifted.

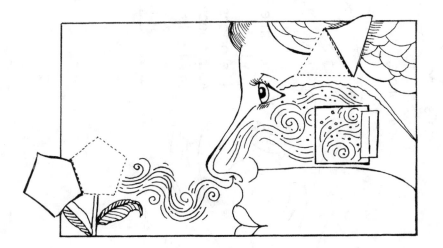

Teaching With the Model

Ask students to name things they like and dislike to smell. Have them read their TAKE A WHIFF models by lifting the numbered flaps. Check for understanding by asking the following questions:

◎ What are odors? (invisible particles called molecules given off by some substances) How do odors reach the nose? (through the air we breathe in)

◎ What detects and recognizes odors? (special smell cells in the upper nose, or olfactory bulb)

Mmm! Mmm! Good!

Prove to your students that smelling affects how food tastes. Have students eat a cookie or cracker as they hold their nostrils shut. Then ask them to take a bite of the same food with their nostrils open. How did the food taste each time? How does their sense of smell affect the taste?

Take a Whiff

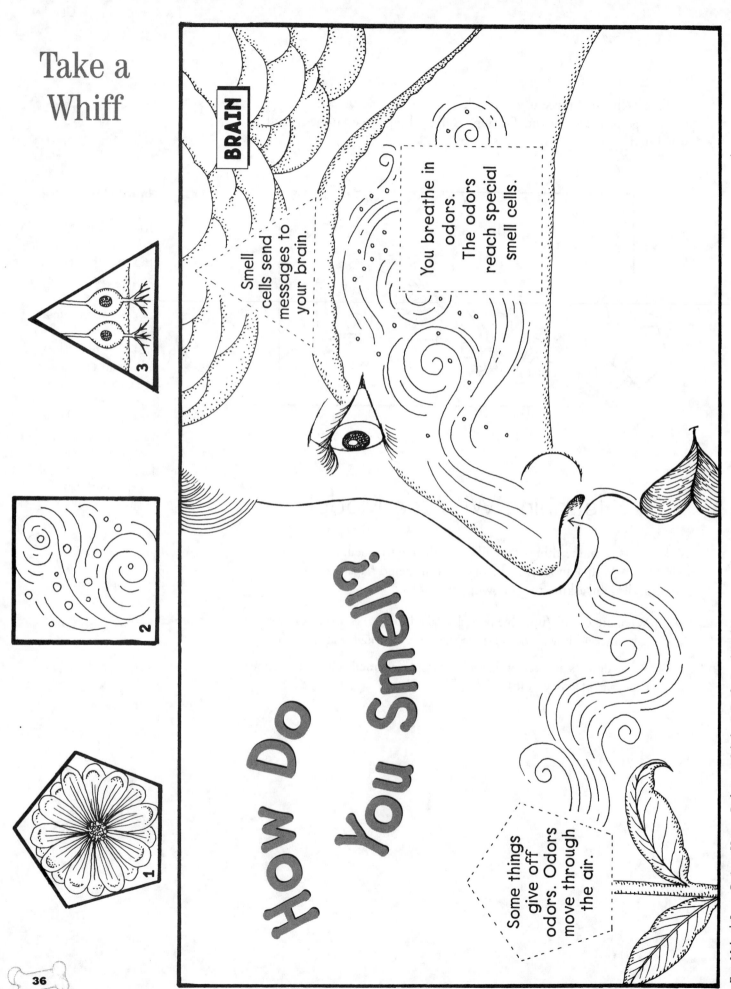

How Do You Smell?

BRAIN

Smell cells send messages to your brain.

You breathe in odors. The odors reach special smell cells.

Some things give off odors. Odors move through the air.

1

2

3

Easy Make & Learn Projects: Human Body   Scholastic Professional Books

Key to Touch (*Touch*)

This movable model illustrates
the sensing nerve endings
of the skin.

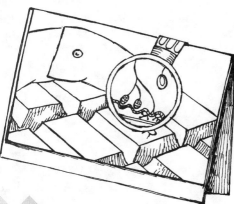

Body Basics

The skin is a nerve-filled sense organ that can detect temperature, pressure, and pain. Different nerve endings detect different sensations and send them to the brain, where they are interpreted.

Making the Model

1 Photocopy page 40. Color the page if desired.

2 Cut out the three pieces along the solid black lines.

3 Fold the construction paper sheet in half, as shown.

Materials

◎ reproducible page 40
◎ 8 1/2-inch by 11-inch sheet of construction paper
◎ brass fasteners
◎ scissors
◎ tape
◎ colored pencils, crayons, or markers (optional)

4 Tape the keyboard piece to one side of the folded construction paper so that the top is flush with the construction paper's center fold.

5 Use the fastener to punch a hole through the black dot on the keyboard piece. It needs to punch through only the top half of the folded paper.

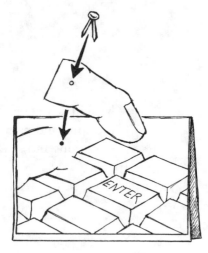

6 Punch the fastener through the black dot on the finger piece. Feed the fastener with the finger piece attached through the hole on the keyboard piece, as shown. Bend back the ends of the fastener from behind to secure it.

7 Fold down the tab on the magnifying glass piece along the dotted line. Tape the tab to the back half of the folded construction paper so the handle of the magnifying glass is centered over the X. Fold the magnifying glass over the back of the model, as shown.

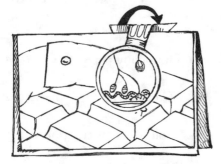

Teaching With the Model

1 Ask students to name objects that feel soft, hard, smooth, rough, hot, or cold. How do they know they feel this way? (Nerve endings in the skin detect these sensations and send the information to the brain.)

2 What happens after the nerve endings sense touch? (Nerves send the messages to the brain.)

3 Have students look at their KEY TO TOUCH models. Have them place the finger above the keyboard and then lower it until it touches the ENTER key. Ask students to flip the magnifying glass over so that it is above the tip of the finger pressing the key. Check for understanding by asking the following questions:

◎ What happens when the finger lightly touches the ENTER key? (Nerve endings labeled A in the epidermis and upper dermis sense light touch.)

◎ What happens when the finger presses down harder on the key? (Nerve endings in the lower part of the dermis labeled B sense more intense pressure.)

Explore More!

What's in the Box?

Challenge students to use only their sense of touch to identify objects hidden from sight. For each pair of students, cut a hole in the side of a shoe box big enough for a student's hand to fit through. Place four or more objects in the box and close the lid. Choose objects that provide a challenge such as cooked spaghetti, a seashell, a bar of soap, a small bowl of dirt or sand, a string of beads, a lemon, marbles, or a pinecone. Invite one student in each pair to slip his or her hand inside the box, feel each object, and try to name it. (Have students keep their guesses a secret by recording them on a piece of paper.) Then have partners take a turn. Afterward, ask: How did your sense of touch help you make guesses? How did it mislead you?

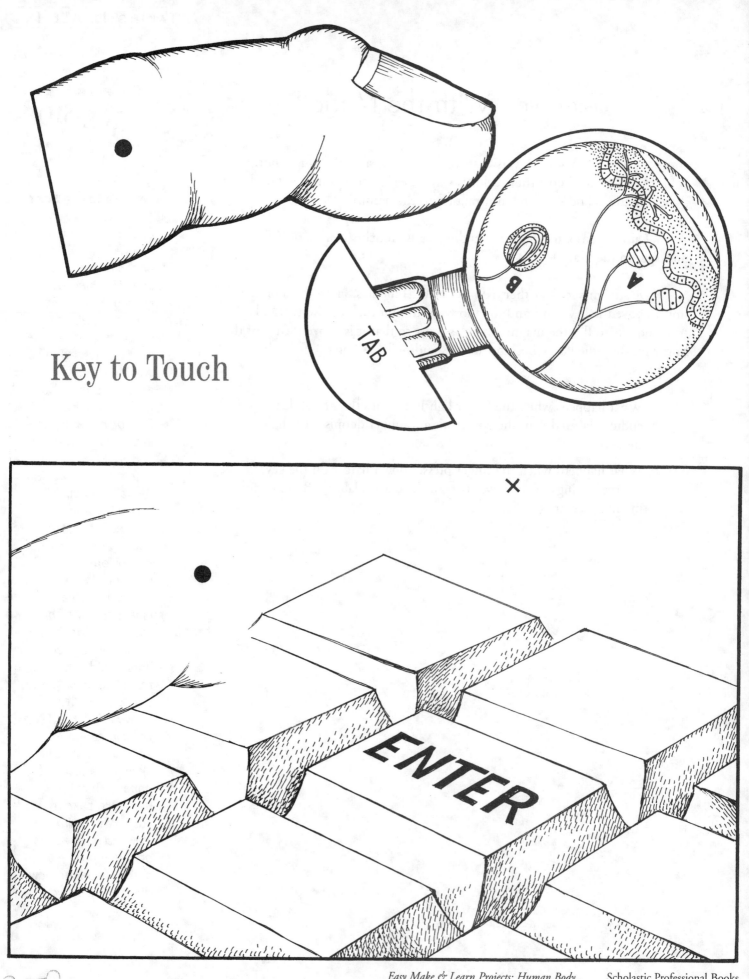

Key to Touch

What's in Skin?

Students make a model
to learn about
the structure of skin.

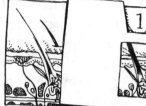

Body Basics

The skin is the largest organ of the body. It accounts for nearly one-sixth of a person's body weight. The skin along with the hair, nails, and sweat glands make up the *integumentary* system. Skin protects the body from outside germs, chemicals, and general wear and tear. Skin also helps control the temperature of the body by sweating.

Skin has two main layers. The top layer, or *epidermis*, is only as thick as a sheet of paper. The cells at the surface are actually dead. They continually flake off as newer cells push up to replace them. The epidermis is the protective part of the skin. It's also where your skin color comes from. The lower layer of the skin, or *dermis*, is much thicker and more complex than the epidermis. The dermis is filled with nerves and sensors that feel pressure and temperature, blood vessels that deliver nutrients to the skin and carry away wastes, glands that produce cooling sweat, glands that make oil that moisturizes the skin and hair, and special hair-growing sacs.

Making the Model

1 Photocopy page 43. Color the page if desired.

2 Cut out the four pieces along the solid black outer lines.

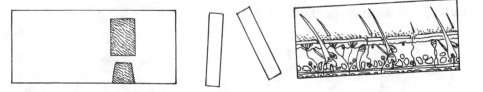

Materials

◎ reproducible page 43
◎ scissors
◎ tape
◎ crayons, colored pencils, or markers (optional)

41

Keep Cool!

• • •

In a patch of skin the size of a postage stamp, there are hundreds of sweat glands. When pores in the skin release sweat, this moisture evaporates on the skin's surface and helps cool us off. Demonstrate this for students with this simple activity. Have them wet the back of one hand with water (to represent sweat on our skin) and leave the other hand dry (to represent our skin if we didn't sweat). Then tell them to blow gently on both hands. Which hand feels cooler?

3 Cut out the two hatch-lined sections on the large rectangular piece that has text written on it.

4 Place this large rectangular piece facedown. Tape the two SUPPORT STRIPS on both sides of the cut-out square, as shown.

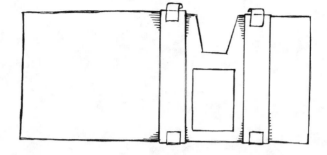

5 Slide the other large rectangular picture piece facedown under the support strips. The numbers should show through at the top cut-out notch, and the picture piece should slide freely.

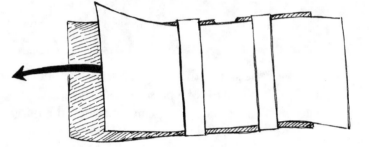

Teaching With the Model

1 Ask students how their skin helps them. (protects, touching/feeling, hair grows out of it, sweats to cool them)

2 Have students use the model to review what's in skin and what it can do by looking at the three illustrations in the box. The text explains what these parts do.

3 Challenge students to name the two layers of the skin (epidermis and dermis) and identify them on the model.

What's in Skin?

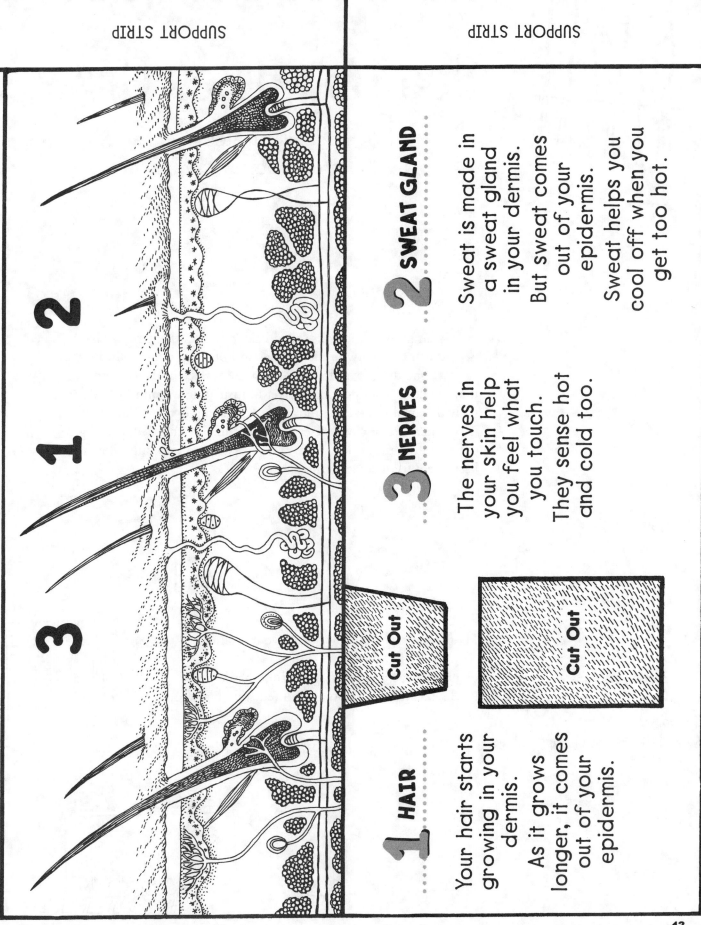

2 SWEAT GLAND

Sweat is made in a sweat gland in your dermis. But sweat comes out of your epidermis. Sweat helps you cool off when you get too hot.

3 NERVES

The nerves in your skin help you feel what you touch. They sense hot and cold too.

Cut Out

Cut Out

1 HAIR

Your hair starts growing in your dermis. As it grows longer, it comes out of your epidermis.

Easy Make & Learn Projects: Human Body   Scholastic Professional Books

See How They Grow

This model illustrates how hair grows out of skin.

Body Basics

Hair grows out of sacs called hair *follicles* in the dermis. Live hair cells grow in the follicles and push up dying cells. By the time the cells in the hair reach the surface of the epidermis, they are dead. Hair provides a layer of insulating warmth for the body. It can also serve as protection. For example, the eyelashes trigger nerves that close the eyelid when they are touched, keeping out harmful dust or dirt. Nose and ear hairs also trap impurities and keep them from entering the body.

Materials

- reproducible page 46
- scissors
- tape
- six 12-inch-long pieces of string
- crayons, colored pencils, or markers (optional)

Making the Model

1 Photocopy page 46. Color the page if desired.

2 Cut the page in half along the solid black center line. Cut the six slots along their solid black lines.

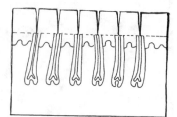

3 Fold the other piece along its dotted line. Tape the two pieces together, as shown.

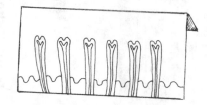
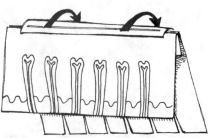

4 Tie the pieces of string together at one end, as shown.

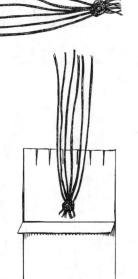

5 Turn the combined model piece face down. Set the string bundle on top of it.

Explore More!

Get a Closer Look

Invite students to get a closer look at their own skin and hair using hand lenses. Have them draw what they see and compare it to their models. If microscopes are available, students can make slides of hair or skin flakes and draw what they see.

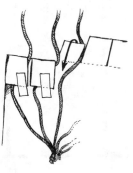

6 Start at the left side. Slide one string through the first slot on the left. Then fold down the far left tab and tape it down. Continue with the second string, slot, fold, and tape, as shown. Repeat until all the strings are threaded through and secured.

7 Fold up the bottom half and tape it to the top half along the sides and between each string, as shown. (See the finished model drawing on page 44.)

Teaching With the Model

1 Ask students about hair. What are its functions? (warmth, lashes protect eyes, nose hairs trap dust and other impurities) Is the hair on their head dead or alive? (dead) Where does hair come from? (the skin's dermis)

2 Have students label the dermis and epidermis on their models and identify the hair follicles. Ask: Where is the hair root? (bottom of follicle) Let students make the hair on their models "grow" by pulling on the strings.

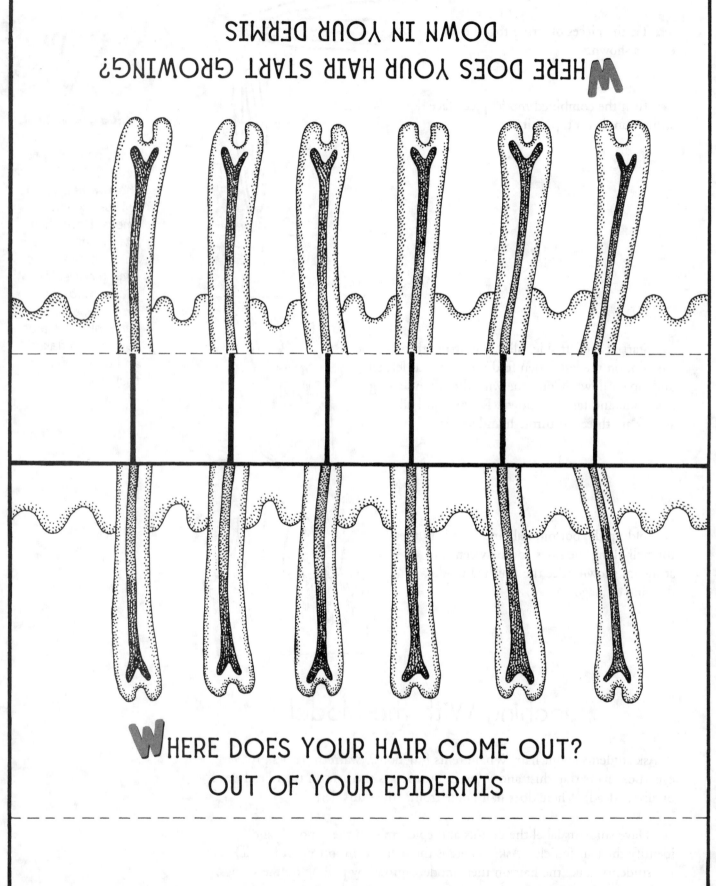

WHERE DOES YOUR HAIR START GROWING?
DOWN IN YOUR DERMIS

WHERE DOES YOUR HAIR COME OUT?
OUT OF YOUR EPIDERMIS

Easy Make & Learn Projects: Human Body

Scholastic Professional Books

Where Are My Bones?

Students make a model of the human skeleton and explore its functions.

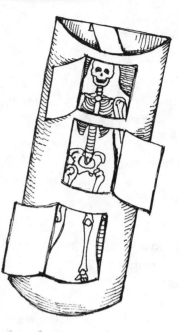

Body Basics

The skeleton is the body's frame. The *skeletal system* is made up of the bones plus the *cartilage* and *ligaments* that join bone to bone at the *joints*. Bones are the strong framework where muscles attach. Without bones and muscles, standing up, running, and lifting wouldn't be possible. Bones also protect the body. The skull protects the brain, and ribs protect the lungs, heart, and other organs.

The bones of the human body come in many different shapes and sizes. Most people have 206 bones in their body, though some have an extra pair of ribs or lack a small bone or two in their hands, feet, or tailbones. The thighbone is the largest bone, and the three bones in the middle ear are the smallest.

Joints allow bending and movement, such as at the elbow, knee, or hip. The way the bones of a joint are connected determines the direction in which those bones can move. A hinge joint, like that at the elbow or knee, allows movement in only two directions whereas the ball-and-socket joint of the hips and shoulders allows for a much wider range of motion. Some joints, like the gliding joints between the vertebrae of the back, allow only a little movement. The bones of joints are attached to each other with strong ligaments and are lined with protective cartilage.

Materials

- reproducible pages 50 and 51
- scissors
- tape
- crayons, colored pencils, or markers (optional)

Making the Model

1 Photocopy pages 50 and 51. Color the pages if desired.

2 Cut along each window's three solid dark lines. Then open the windows by folding each on its dotted lines.

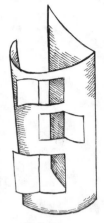

3 Fold page 50 back along its long vertical dotted line. Tape the two edges of the page together, as shown.

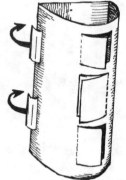

4 Cut out the five pieces on page 51 along the solid black lines.

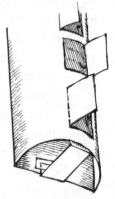

5 Take SUPPORT STRIP A and fold the front and back tabs faceup along the dotted lines. Tape the back tab to the bottom back of the WHERE ARE MY BONES? piece and the front tab to its front, as shown. This adds support to the model.

6 Challenge students to figure out where the missing bones belong on the skeleton and tape them on.

7 Take SUPPORT STRIP B and fold the front and back tabs faceup along the dotted lines, as in step 5.

8 Fold the tab on the top of the skeleton back along the dotted line. Tape this tab to SUPPORT STRIP B where indicated. Make sure the FRONT tab is in front of the skeleton.

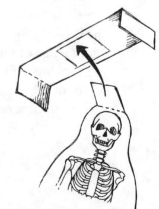

9 Lower the skeleton inside the model's top and tape the back tab to the top back of the model, as shown.

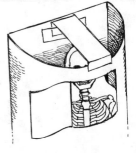

10 Either tape the front tab to the top front of the model or hook the front tab over the front lip of the model. Not taping will allow students to lift out their skeletons if they choose.

Teaching With the Model

1 Ask students what gives their bodies shape. (the bones of their skeleton) Invite students to look at the WHERE ARE MY BONES? model and name as many bones as they can. (Students may lift out their skeletons to label the bones.)

2 Ask: Where are the longest bones in the body? (legs)

3 Where are some of the shortest? (hands, feet, or back; note that the smallest bones in the body, the middle ear bones, cannot be seen in the model)

4 Have students study their model as they feel some of the bones in their body (collarbone, cervical vertebrae at the back of the neck, shinbone, and so on).

5 Challenge students to define a joint and name some of the joints in the model. (elbow, hip, shoulder, knee, and so on)

6 Ask: What do joints do? (connect bone to bone and allow movement)

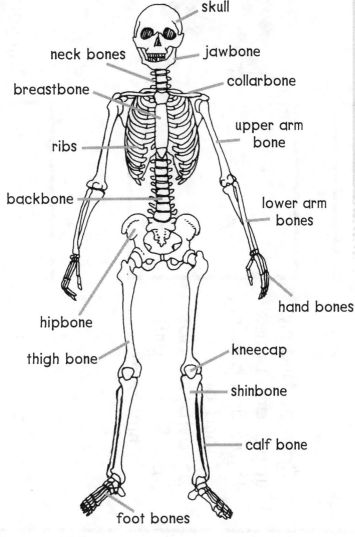

Labels on the skeleton diagram: skull, neck bones, jawbone, breastbone, collarbone, ribs, upper arm bone, backbone, lower arm bones, hipbone, hand bones, thigh bone, kneecap, shinbone, calf bone, foot bones

Explore More!

Stand Up!

What if we didn't have a skeleton? Help your students find out with this activity. Invite them to use clay to make figures with long thin torsos, arms, and legs. Do their figures stand up? (no) Challenge students to find a way to make their figures stand up. Have straws, toothpicks, or dried pasta on hand. Students can remold their figures around these materials to discover how an internal skeleton adds support to their bodies.

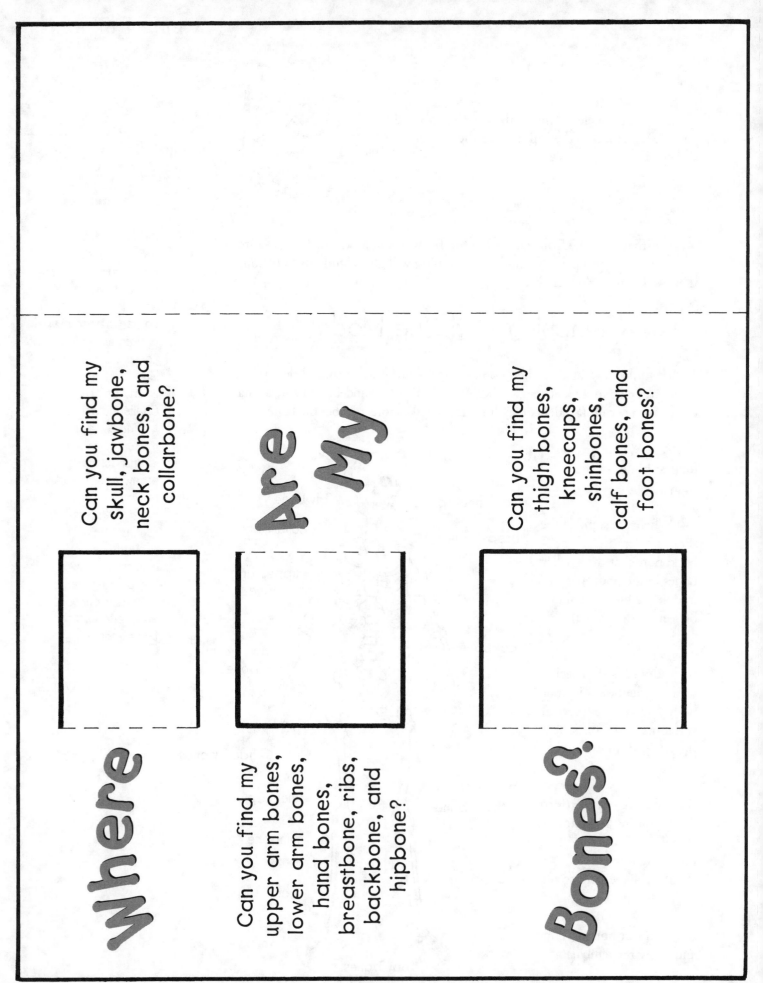

Can you find my skull, jawbone, neck bones, and collarbone?

Are
My

Can you find my thigh bones, kneecaps, shinbones, calf bones, and foot bones?

Where

Can you find my upper arm bones, lower arm bones, hand bones, breastbone, ribs, backbone, and hipbone?

Bones?

Where Are My Bones?   *Easy Make & Learn Projects: Human Body*   Scholastic Professional Books

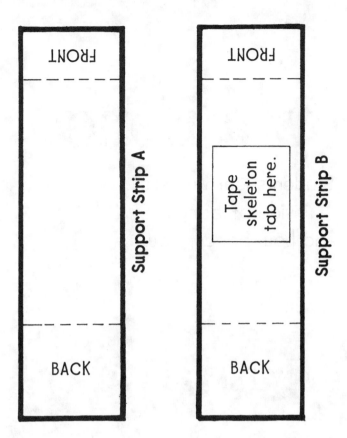

FRONT

Support Strip A

BACK

FRONT

Tape
skeleton
tab here.

Support Strip B

BACK

Where Are My Bones?

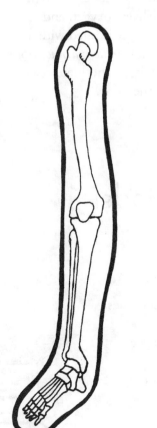 

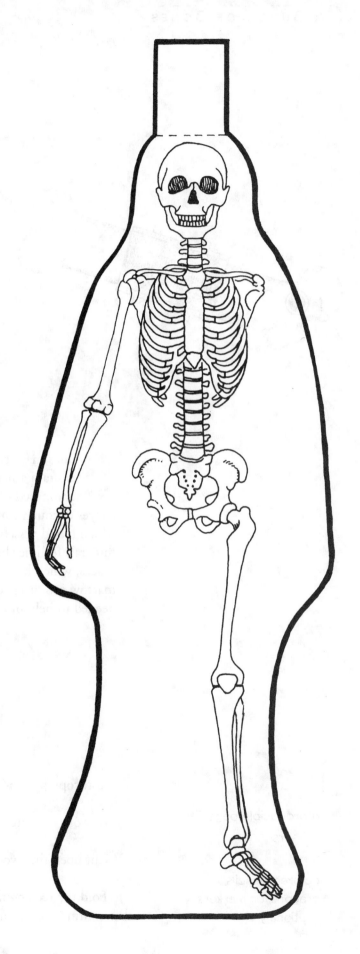

Grow a Bone

Students learn what's inside of bones and how bones grow.

Body Basics

Bones may seem hard as rock, but they are living tissue that contain a network of blood vessels and nerves. Most bones are composed of layers. An outer skinlike white membrane covers a layer of tough *compact bone*. It contains canals or tubes through which blood vessels and nerves run. Blood delivers oxygen and minerals to inner bone cells. The *spongy bone* layer is filled with air spaces, which help make bones light and contain *bone marrow*. Bone marrow produces red blood cells that carry oxygen and platelets needed to help blood clot, and stores fat for the body.

Materials

- reproducible page 54
- scissors
- tape
- colored pencils, crayons, or markers (optional)

Making the Model

1 Photocopy page 54. Color the page if desired.

2 Cut out the three pieces along the solid black lines.

3 Cut open the two slits on the rectangular piece.

4 Fold the rectangular piece along the dotted lines that continue out from the slits.

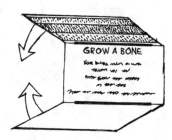

5 Turn over the rectangular piece. Turn one of the bone pieces over and fit it into the slits, as shown.

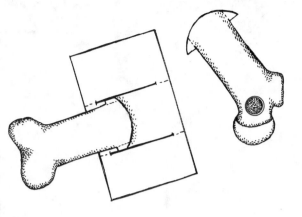

6 Repeat step 5 with the other bone piece.

7 Fold the flaps of the rectangular piece so that the INSIDE BONE label and picture show. Tape the top flap down, as shown.

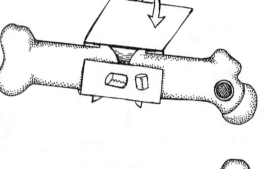

8 Fold down the small triangular parts of the bone pieces that extend out of the slits. Turn the model over and push the two bone pieces together as far as they will go.

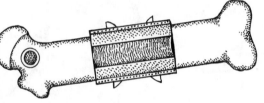

Teaching With the Model

1 Ask students if they think their bones are dead or living tissue. (living) How do they know? (broken bones heal, bones grow)

2 Invite students to pull both ends of the GROW A BONE model out very slowly until the bone has "grown" to its full size. Explain that bones can grow at both ends and in diameter.

3 Ask students to turn their models over and look at the bone cutaway. Discuss the characteristics and functions of each inside part.

Explore More!

Building Strong Bones

Calcium provides the building material for bones and teeth, making them hard. Since bones continue to grow and develop up to early adulthood, an adequate intake of calcium is necessary for bones to build on. Try this activity to demonstrate the importance of calcium to our bones. Place a clean, cooked chicken bone in a jar filled with vinegar and cover it. Place another bone on a paper towel. After a week, remove the bone from the jar. Ask: How did the bone change? How does it compare to the bone left on the paper towel? (Vinegar, an acid, leaches the calcium out of the bone, making it soft and rubbery. Point out to students, however, that when we ingest vinegar, it does not affect our bones.)

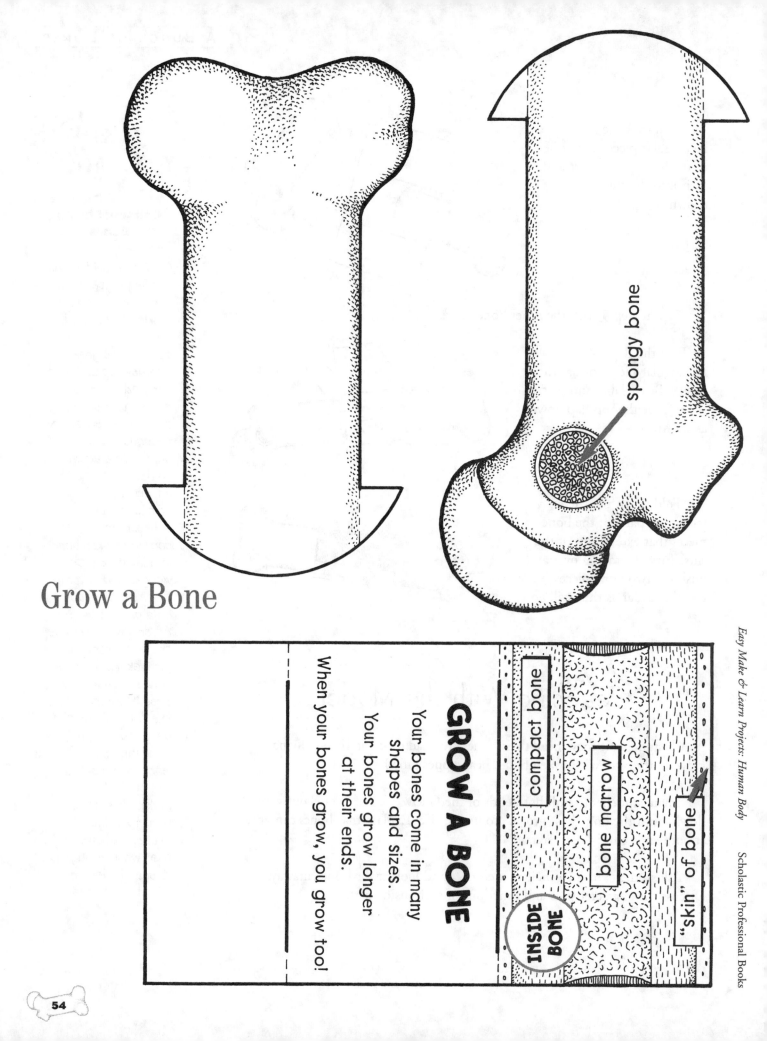

Grow a Bone

spongy bone

GROW A BONE

Your bones come in many
shapes and sizes.
Your bones grow longer
at their ends.

When your bones grow, you grow too!

compact bone

bone marrow

INSIDE BONE

"skin" of bone

Easy Make & Learn Projects: Human Body   Scholastic Professional Books

Muscle Maker

Students make a model that shows how muscles pull on bones.

Body Basics

Muscles are what move the body. The *muscular system* is made up of more than 600 individual muscles. Muscles attach to the bones they move with stringy *tendons*. Some muscles move under our direction, like arm and leg muscles. These are voluntary, or *skeletal* muscles. Skeletal muscle tissue is made up of bundled muscle fibers, which are in turn made up of long, striped muscle cells. Other muscles work by themselves. Organ and blood vessel muscles are examples of involuntary, or *smooth* muscles. *Cardiac*, or heart muscle has characteristics of both of smooth and skeletal muscle.

Skeletal muscles work by contracting, or shortening, and then relaxing, or lengthening. When you "make a muscle," the muscle in your upper arm (the biceps) contracts and shortens and thickens into a bulge. This bends the elbow and pulls the bones of the arm toward each other. When you relax the muscle, it lengthens and the arm unbends at the elbow. Nerves send signals to muscles that make them relax or contract. The nerves carry messages from the brain. Skeletal muscles can be controlled just by thinking about them. Smooth and heart muscle cannot.

Making the Model

Materials

- reproducible page 57
- scissors
- 2 brass fasteners
- crayons, colored pencils, or markers (optional)

1 Photocopy page 57. Color the page if desired.

2 Cut out the three pieces along the solid black lines.

Muscle Power

• • •

Many of our muscles work in pairs: When one muscle contracts, the other muscle relaxes. Ask students to put one hand, palm up, against the underside of the their desk and push upward. With their other hand, have them feel the front and back of their upper arm. Ask: Did the muscle in front or back get hard? Explain that the hard muscle in the front is called the *biceps*. When it bunches up, the muscle in the back of the arm (the *triceps*) relaxes. Now have students press on the desktop with their palm and feel their muscles again. What happens? (The triceps contracts and hardens and the biceps relaxes and softens.) Challenge students to find out whether their leg muscles work in the same way.

3 Cut open the slit along the solid black line of the upper arm piece. Punch holes at the four black dots using the tip of the scissors or the fasteners.

4 Set the two arm pieces at right angles to each other with the lower arm on top. Feed one fastener through the lower arm's end hole and the upper arm's hole, as shown.

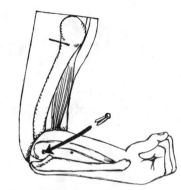

5 Set the muscle piece behind the arm pieces. Match up its hole to the other hole of the lower arm and feed the second fastener through. Fold back the fastener's ends.

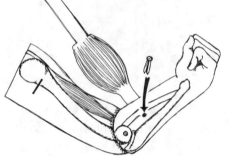

6 Slide the end of the muscle labeled PULL through the slit so it can be pulled from the front of the model.

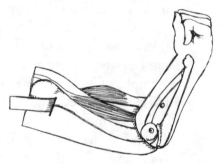

Teaching With the Model

1 Ask students to make a muscle by bending their elbows. Then ask them to work the model by pulling up on the PULL tab to contract the muscle and then pulling down on the lower arm to relax the muscle. Ask them to describe the process.

2 Ask students if muscles pull or push—or both. (only pull)

3 Challenge students to name what kind of muscle makes the arm move. (skeletal muscle)

4 Ask: What are the three kinds of muscle and where are they found? (skeletal muscle in muscles you move yourself; smooth muscle in organs and blood vessels; heart, or cardiac muscle in the heart)

Muscle Maker

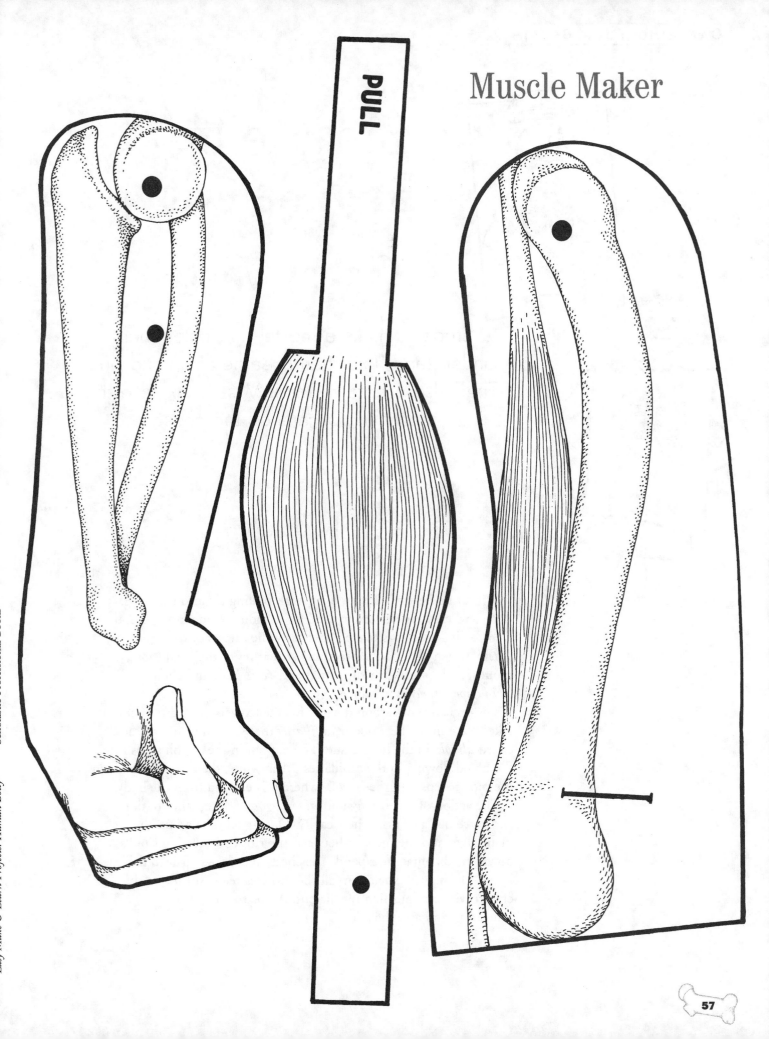

PULL

Easy Make & Learn Projects: Human Body   Scholastic Professional Books

Breathe In, Breathe Out

Chest Vest

Students make a model that helps them understand how they breathe air in and out. They also create a Chest Vest to explore the breathing organs of the chest.

Body Basics

Our bodies are constantly at work pulling air into the *lungs*, where oxygen is exchanged for carbon dioxide in the blood. This process is made possible by the organs of the *respiratory system*, which include the breathing structures of the head (nose, mouth, and *sinuses*), throat (throat and *voice box*), and chest (*windpipe*, *bronchi*, and lungs).

The exchange of carbon dioxide for the oxygen needed to fuel cells takes place in the network of *capillaries* that surround tiny air sacs, called *alveoli*, in the lung tissue. The oxygen in the alveoli seeps into the blood flowing in the capillaries. Meanwhile, the carbon dioxide in the blood seeps into the alveoli, where it is exhaled from the body.

The action of the *ribcage* and *diaphragm* work together to draw in and force out air in the chest cavity. During an inhalation, the diaphragm and the muscles between the ribs contract. This pulls down the diaphragm, expands the chest, and draws air into the lungs. During an exhalation, all the muscles relax, shrinking the chest cavity and pushing the air out. A breath consists of an inhalation and an exhalation.

✂ Making the Models

Breathe In, Breathe Out

Materials

◎ reproducible page 60
◎ scissors
◎ tape
◎ crayons, colored pencils, or markers (optional)

1 Photocopy page 60. Color the page if desired.

2 Cut out the four pieces along the solid black lines.

3 There are four solid black cut lines on the piece that pictures the boy: two short slots, a long straight one, and a curved one. Cut them all open.

4 Fold the tabs of the two rib pieces back along the dotted lines.

5 Slide the tab of rib piece A into the short slot on the left.

6 Repeat step 5 with rib piece B and the short slot on the right. Turn the model over and tape down both tabs, as shown. Turn the model back over and press the ribs down over the lungs.

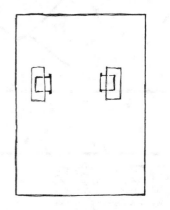

7 Pinch together the BREATHE IN end of the long piece, as shown, and insert it into the straight slot.

8 Pull the long piece through the top slot from the back and feed it out through the curved slot. Smooth out the long piece. (See the finished model drawing on page 58.)

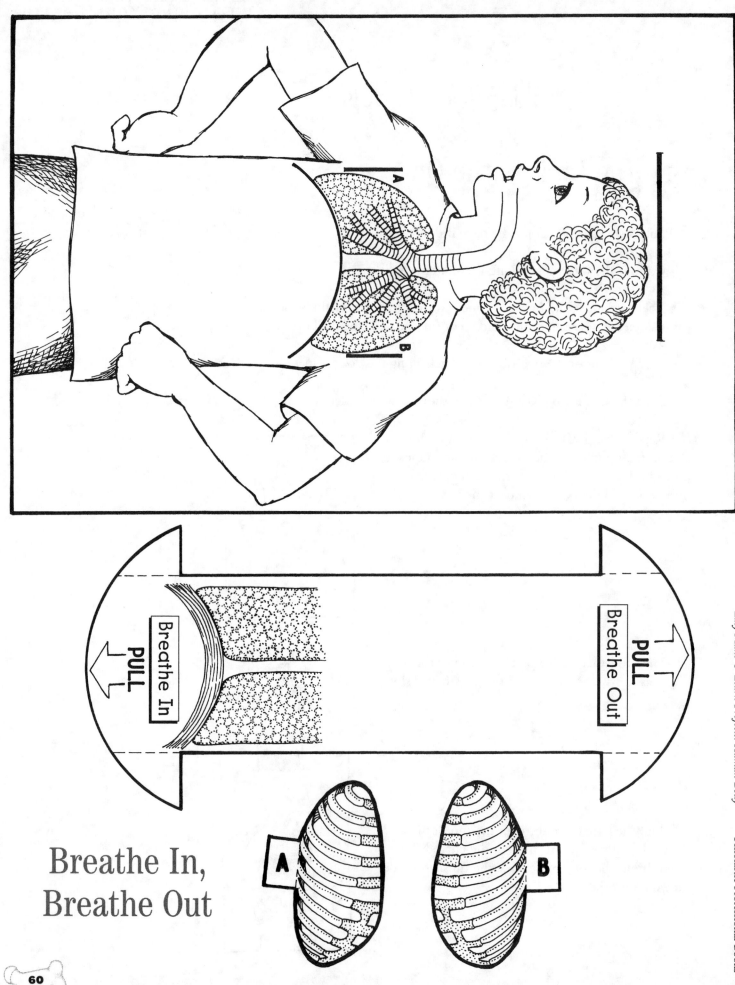

Breathe In, Breathe Out

Breathe Out
PULL

Breathe In
PULL

A

B

Easy Make & Learn Projects: Human Body

Scholastic Professional Books

Chest Vest

1 Photocopy pages 63 and 64. Color the pages if desired.

2 Cut out the five pieces along the dark solid lines.

3 Use paper bags or brown craft paper to create "ponchos" for the students. If using grocery bags, cut a hole for the head in the bottom as well as armholes in the sides. If using a sheet of craft paper, fold it in half and cut a hole for the head.

Materials

◎ reproducible pages 63 and 64
◎ brown paper grocery bags or 16- by 36-inch sheets of brown craft paper
◎ scissors
◎ tape
◎ colored pencils, crayons, or markers (optional)

  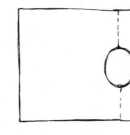

4 Place the WINDPIPE/AIR SACS piece on the front of the poncho so that the windpipe ends at the hole for the head. Tape it down only at the tab and across the top of the windpipe.

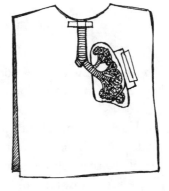

5 Place the OUTSIDE OF LUNG piece so that the cut windpipe end lines up with the WINDPIPE piece, as shown. Tape the OUTSIDE OF LUNG piece down only at its tab.

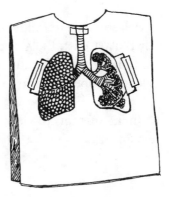

(continued on next page)

Counting Breaths

Invite students to compare their breathing rate at rest and during exercise. Have partners count the number of complete breaths (an inhalation and exhalation) they take in 60 seconds. Then have the students do 30 jumping jacks and count again. Did the number of breaths increase? Why? (Muscles need more oxygen during exercise.)

6 Tape the two RIBS pieces by their tabs so that they fit over the lungs and meet.

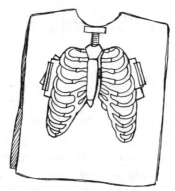

7 Open the RIBS, lift up the WINDPIPE and OUTSIDE OF LUNG pieces, and tape the HEART piece under them, as shown.

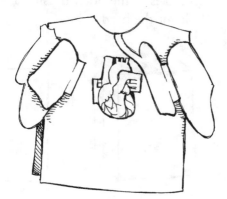

Teaching With the Models

1 Ask students to take a deep breath with a hand over their chests. What happens? (Chest rises when they breathe in and falls when they breathe out.)

2 Have students pull down on the tab on their BREATHE IN, BREATHE OUT models. Ask: What do you see? (curved diaphragm muscle drops) Every time we inhale, the diaphragm moves down and flattens. Now ask them to lift the ribs. Are the lungs full or empty of air? (full) Have students pull up on the tab, lift the ribs, and compare what happens to the diaphragm and size of the lungs.

3 Ask students to follow the path of air from the mouth to the lungs on their BREATHE IN, BREATHE OUT models. Challenge them to name the breathing structures of the head, throat, and chest along the way. Invite students to label these structures on their model.

4 Invite students to wear their CHEST VESTS. Have pairs of students trace the path air takes with their finger on their partner's vest.

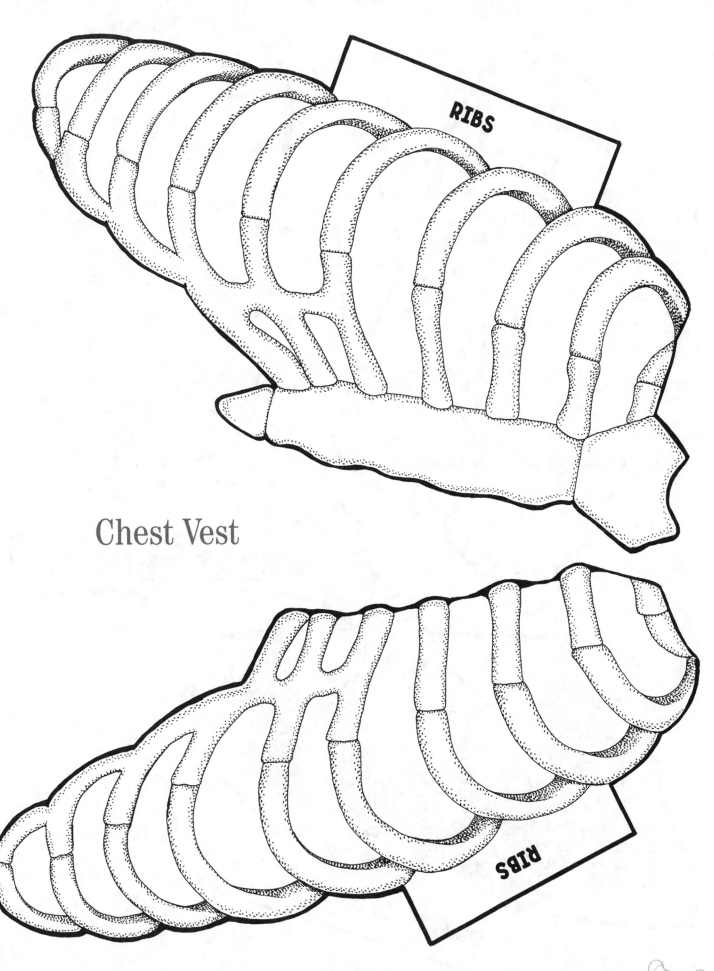

RIBS

Chest Vest

RIBS

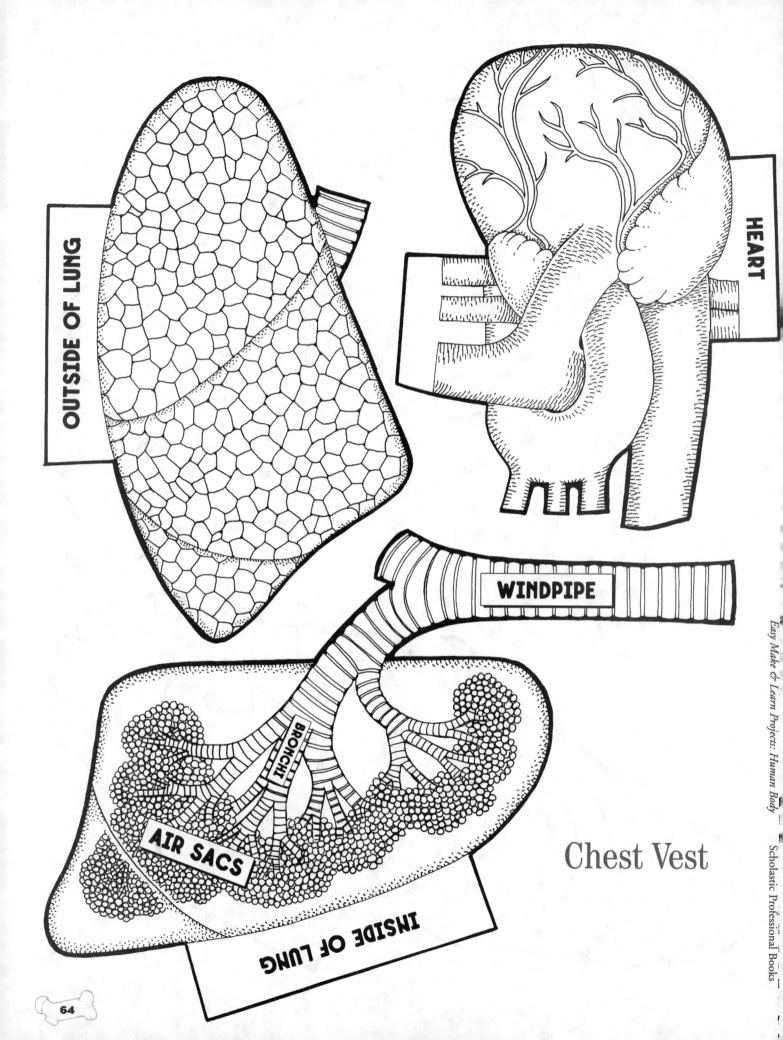

OUTSIDE OF LUNG

HEART

WINDPIPE

BRONCHI

AIR SACS

INSIDE OF LUNG

Chest Vest

Easy Make & Learn Projects: Human Body Scholastic Professional Books

Have a Heart

· · · · · · · · · · · · · · ·

Circulation Wheel

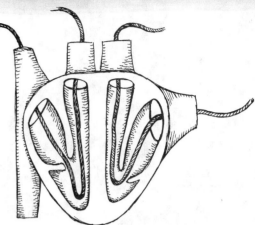

Students make a model of the heart that shows its four chambers and the route blood takes. They also assemble a wheel that illustrates how blood circulates around the body.

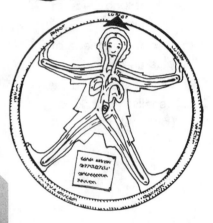

Body Basics

The job of the *circulatory* system is to supply oxygen and food to every cell of the body via the blood. The circulatory system is made up of the body's blood pumping organ (the heart), the blood, and blood vessels in which blood travels.

In the center of the chest between the lungs is the *heart*, a four-chambered, mostly hollow muscle that squeezes every second or so. The heart receives blood from the veins and pumps it though the arteries. The heart has two sides, left and right. Blood depleted of oxygen comes into the right side of the heart. From there it is pumped to the lungs, where it picks up oxygen and returns to the heart's left side and is pumped out to the body. The heart is an amazing organ, pumping thousands of gallons of blood every day over a lifetime.

Blood is a liquid mixture of water, red and white blood cells, minerals, mineral salts, enzymes, hormones, and food for cells and tissues (fats, sugars, and proteins). Besides delivering needed food and oxygen to cells, blood picks up wastes, like carbon dioxide. Blood cells are produced in the bones, and dead ones are removed by the spleen and liver.

Materials

- reproducible page 67
- scissors
- tape
- 3-foot-long piece of red yarn
- 3-foot-long piece of blue yarn
- crayons, colored pencils, or markers (optional)

Making the Models

Have a Heart

1 Photocopy page 67. Color the pages if desired.

2 Cut out the heart along the solid black lines. Then cut out the four hatch-lined ovals.

3 Hold one end of the blue yarn behind the far left FROM BODY hole and thread it through. Then feed in through the TO LUNGS hole. Allow equal amounts of slack to hang out of each hole.

4 Tape down the yarn, as shown.

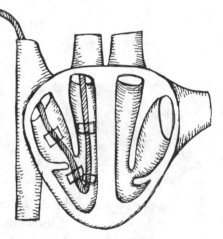

5 Repeat steps 3 and 4 with the red yarn and the right side. Students will later tie the yarns as part of the Teaching With the Model activity.)

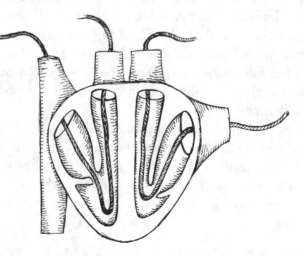

Have a Heart

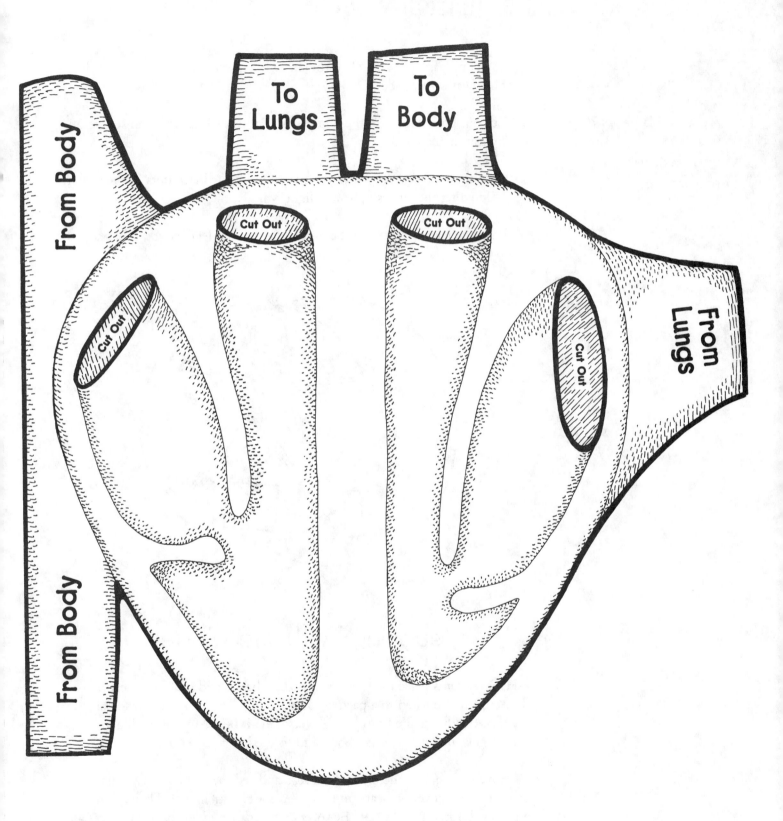

Materials

- reproducible pages 70 and 71
- brass fasteners
- scissors
- tape
- red and blue colored pencils, crayons, or markers

Circulation Wheel

1 Photocopy pages 70 and 71. (Students will color the model as part of the Teaching With the Model activity.)

2 Cut out both circles on the two pages. Cut out the hatch-lined square on the slightly smaller circle.

3 Place the smaller circle on top of the larger so the black dots in the centers meet. (Holding the circles up to the light will help.)

4 Push the fastener through the dots. Turn the model over and fold back the ends of the fastener.

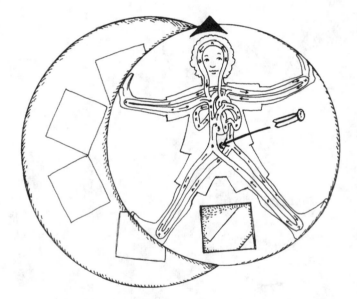

Teaching With the Models

1 Have students place their hands over their hearts and feel them beating (or allow students to listen to a partner's heart using a cardboard paper towel tube). Ask: What is the heart doing every time it beats? (pumping blood) Why? (move blood out to the body and to the lungs to get oxygen)

2 Have students tie the blue TO LUNGS and red FROM LUNGS ends of the yarn together above the heart on their HAVE A HEART model. Then ask them to tie the TO BODY and FROM BODY ends together and let this lung loop hang down in front of the heart.

3 Discuss the terms *oxygen-rich* and *oxygen-poor*. (Blood that is full of oxygen is oxygen-rich; blood that has been depleted of oxygen is oxygen-poor.) Help students trace the path of oxygen-rich blood (red yarn) and oxygen-poor blood. (blue yarn)

4 Ask: Is blood coming from the body oxygen-rich or oxygen-poor? (oxygen-poor) What about blood going to the lungs? (oxygen-poor) Where does blood get oxygen? (lungs)

5 Ask students to hold the model over their chest. Ask: Which side of the heart pumps oxygen-poor blood to the lungs? (right) Which side pumps oxygen-rich blood out to the body? (left)

6 Invite students to read their CIRCULATION WHEEL models by turning the wheels.

7 Ask students why blood needs to circulate around the body. (deliver oxygen and nutrients to every body cell and pick up wastes)

Organ Search

Challenge student groups to choose one of the organs listed on the CIRCULATION WHEEL and find out more about it. Where is it located in the body? how big is it? what does it do? and so on. Students can draw their organs on a classroom outline of the body.

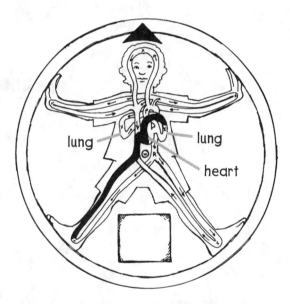

lung   lung

heart

8 Have students color the model. Instruct them to take a blue crayon, pencil, or marker and start on the word BLUE on the boy's right ankle. Have them continue to color the path of blood blue (representing oxygen-poor blood) until they come to an X. At an X they change to a red marker or crayon (representing oxygen-rich blood). Students need to switch colors each time they encounter an X. The small R's (red) and B's (blue) along the way will assist them.

9 Challenge students to point out where the heart and lungs are on their models. How can they tell? (Blood changes direction at the heart; oxygen-poor "blue" blood becomes oxygen-rich "red" blood at the lungs.)

Circulation Wheel
(Top)

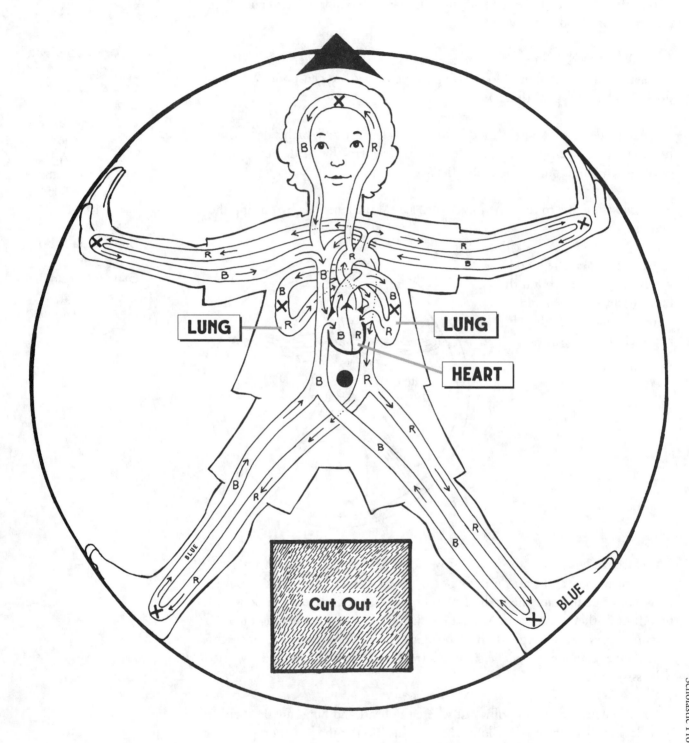

Easy Make & Learn Projects: Human Body
Scholastic Professional Books

Circulation Wheel
(Bottom)

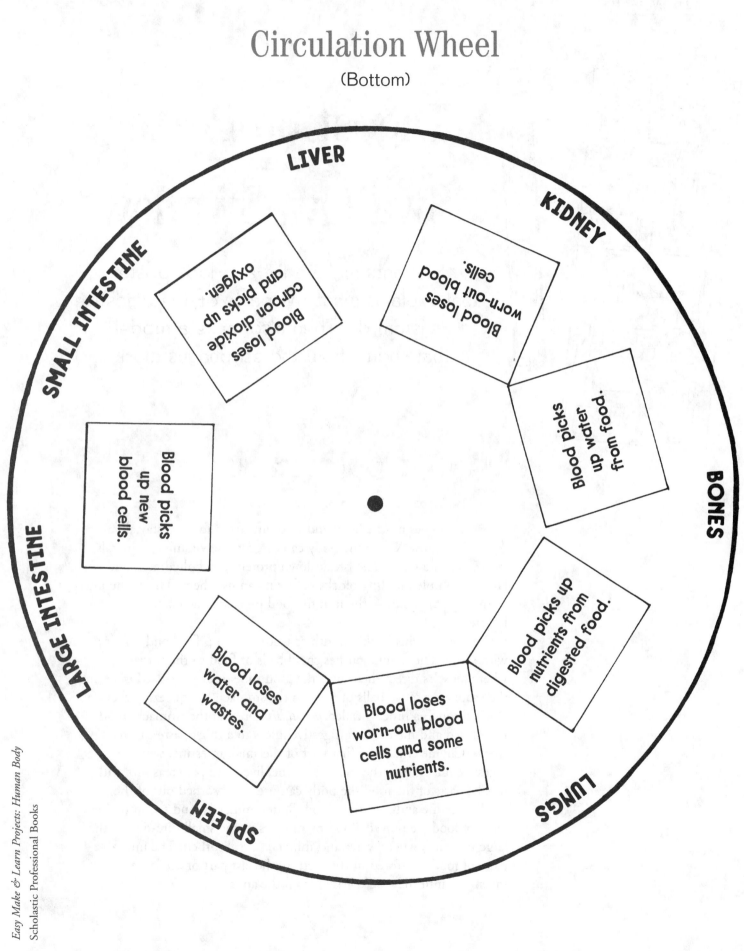

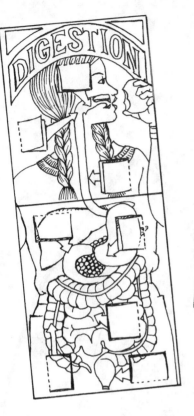

Digestion Poster
....
Swallow, Swallow

Students make a lift-and-look poster that explains what the parts of the digestive system do. They also make a model that shows how the esophagus works.

Body Basics

Our bodies need energy and nutrients from food to stay alive and grow. While the body can directly use vitamins, minerals, and water, it must break down proteins, carbohydrates, and fats into simple building blocks before it can use them. This is the job of the *digestive system*—the mouth, food pipe, stomach, and intestines.

Digestion begins in the mouth as teeth break up food and mix it with saliva. The tongue pushes small balls of food to the throat, where muscles direct them into the food tube or *esophagus*. Muscles in the esophagus move balls of food to the stomach by squeezing them along through a process called *peristalsis*. Once in the stomach, food is churned and mixed with digestive juices to a thick paste called *chyme*. Chyme enters the first part of the small intestine, where digestive juices from the small intestine, liver, and pancreas mix with it. The parts of the food the body can use are absorbed out of the small intestine and into the blood. Water, minerals, and the unusable parts of food are moved along by muscles in the small intestine to the large intestine, where water and minerals are absorbed. The unusable parts of food are stored in the rectum, the last part of the large intestine, until they are released from the anus.

✂ Making the Models

Digestion Poster

1 Photocopy pages 74–77. Color the pages if desired.

2 Cut the border off the top of page 75 along the solid black line. Try to cut off all of the line.

3 Overlap the top of page 75 onto page 74, where indicated. Line up the cut-off top with the dotted line and tape (or glue) the page in place.

4 Repeat steps 2 and 3 for pages 76 and 77.

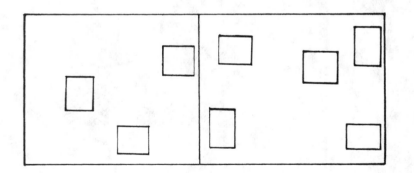

5 Cut open the eight flaps on the illustrated sheet along the solid black lines.

6 Place the illustrated sheet on top of the other sheet. Tape the sheets together at the top, sides, and bottom.

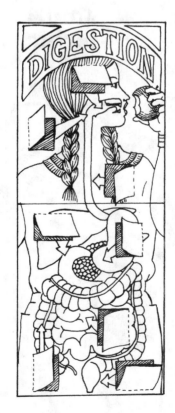

Glue or tape page 75 here.

Digestion Poster

Easy Make & Learn Projects: Human Body   Scholastic Professional Books

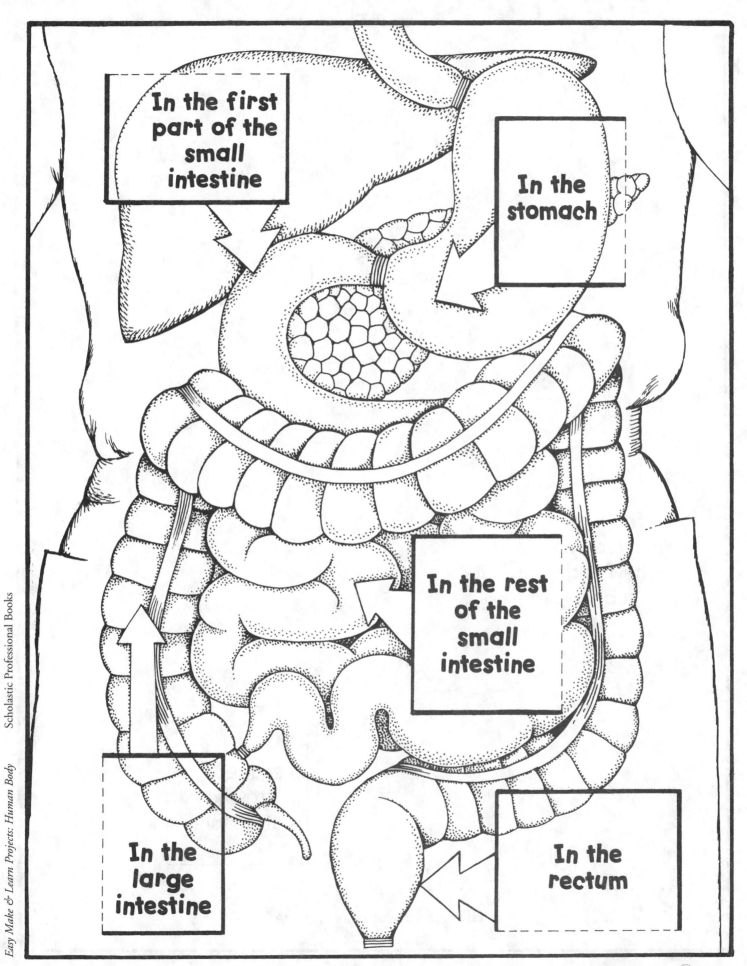

In the first part of the small intestine

In the stomach

In the rest of the small intestine

In the large intestine

In the rectum

Digestion Poster

Easy Make & Learn Projects: Human Body   Scholastic Professional Books

food is
chewed.
Saliva mixes
with it.

food is
moved to
the food
tube.

food is
squeezed
to the
stomach.

Glue or tape page 77 here.

Easy Make & Learn Projects: Human Body   Scholastic Professional Books

Digestion Poster

Intestinal juices
mix with food
and digest it.

food is
mashed
and churned
to paste.
Stomach
juices
mix with it.

digestion
is complete.
Some nutrients
are
absorbed.

the rest
of the
nutrients
are
absorbed.

unusable parts
of the food
are stored until
released from
the body.

Digestion Poster

Materials

- reproducible page 79
- scissors
- 5-inch square of scrap paper
- tape
- colored pencils, crayons, or markers (optional)

Explore More!

A Jelly Donut's Journey

Challenge students to write the story of the path a jelly donut—or other favorite food—takes as it's eaten and digested. Challenge older students to separate how and where in the digestive system the different nutrients in the food (carbohydrates, fats, vitamins, and so on) are broken down and absored.

Swallow, Swallow

1 Photocopy page 79. Color the page if desired.

2 Cut out the piece along the solid black lines.

3 Roll the rectangle into a tube so that the white section is overlapped to the dotted line, as shown. Tape the tube together.

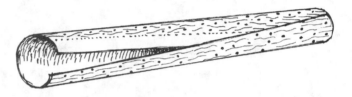

4 Tightly wad up the square of paper into a ball.

Teaching With the Models

1 Ask students what happens to the food they eat. Then invite them to read the DIGESTION POSTER by opening the flaps.

2 Check for understanding about the process by asking questions such as, Where does digestion begin? (mouth) Where are nutrients absorbed into the body? (intestines), and so on.

3 Make additional copies of pages 74–77. Create cards of the text and label boxes and invite students to play Digestion Concentration.

4 Ask students to place balls of paper into their SWALLOW, SWALLOW models. Then have them squeeze the paper along by pinching the tube behind it until the paper comes out the other end. Ask them to describe what they think the model is illustrating. (chewed balls of food being moved down the esophagus or food pipe to the stomach by peristalsis) Have them work the model a number of times.

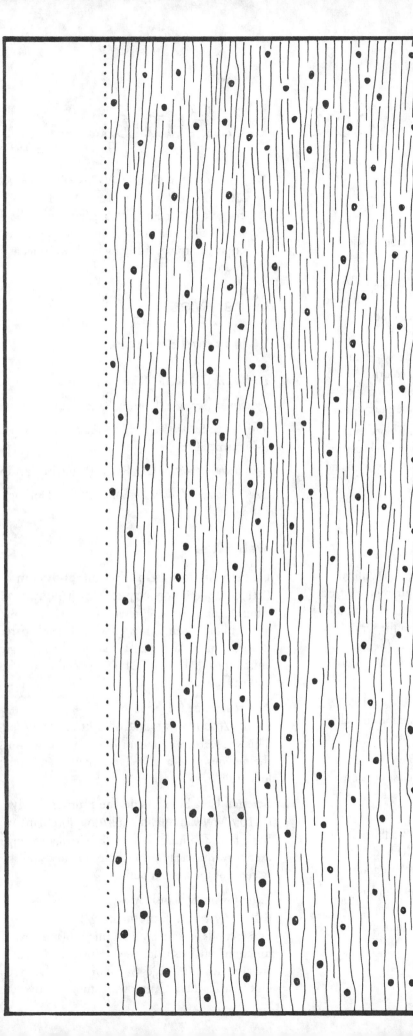

Swallow, Swallow

Resources About the Human Body

Books for Teachers

The Body Atlas by Steve Parker (Dorling Kindersley, 1993). An oversized book that illustrates and labels the structures of the human body.

The Body Book by Donald M. Silver and Patricia J. Wynne (Scholastic, 1993). With just scissors, paste, and paper, you and your students can create paper models of the major organs and systems of the human body.

Human Body by the editors of Time-Life Books (Time-Life, 1992). This book is packed with colorful graphics and uses a question and answer format to discuss the anatomy and function of the human body.

Structure & Function of the Body by Gary A. Thibodeau (Mosby Year Book, 1992). A thorough and exhaustive textbook on the human body that is clearly written and well illustrated.

Books for Students

Bones: Our Skeletal System by Seymour Simon (William Morrow, 1998). Fascinating close-up photographs and illustrations give young readers an inside look at bones and how they function. Other books in the series include: *The Brain: Our Nervous System*, *The Heart: Our Circulatory System*, and *Muscles: Our Muscular System*.

Cells Are Us by Fran Balkwill (Carolrhoda Books, 1993). This fun to read book explains the functions of cells in the human body with lively illustrations.

The Magic School Bus: Inside the Human Body by Joanna Cole (Scholastic, 1989). Ms. Frizzle's class goes on a guided tour of the human body. Also check out *The Magic School Bus Explores the Senses*.

Outside and Inside You by Sandra Markle (Bradbury Press, 1991). Discusses the various parts of the body and their functions with lots of high-tech photographs.

Through the Microscope: The Body by Lionel Bender (Gloucester Press, 1989). Text and microscopic photographs introduce the parts of the human body and its systems.

Why Does My Nose Run? (And Other Questions Kids Ask About Their Bodies) by Joanne Settel and Nancy Baggett (Atheneum, 1985). A fact-filled book about fun phenomena of the human body, such as blinking, crying, burping, shivering, and sweating, as well as goose bumps, dizziness, and more.

Other Media

Videos and Software

Body Park CD-ROM (Virtual Entertainment)

Eyewitness Skeleton (Dorling Kindersley)

The Magic School Bus Explores the Human Body CD-ROM (Microsoft Home)

3-D Body Adventure CD-ROM (Knowledge Adventure)

The Ultimate Human Body CD-ROM (Dorling Kindersley)

Web Sites

Human Anatomy Online-Innerbody.com (http://www.innerbody.com/htm/body.html)
Thumbnail pictures representing the ten systems of the human body open to images with clickable parts that describe them. Also available are a number of great animations that illustrate body functions such as inhaling and exhaling.

Neuroscience for Kids (http://faculty.washington.edu/chudler/neurok.html)
This site features abundant information and images about the nervous system as well as activities, experiments, and lots of links.

Science Fact File: Inside the Human Body (http://www.imcpl.lib.in.us/nov_ind.htm)
Basic facts and images about the circulatory, digestive, excretory, muscular, nervous, respiratory, and skeletal systems of the human body.

Your Gross & Cool Body (http://www.yucky.com/body/)
Fun factoids and wacky scientific explanations of body functions, such as belches, vomit, zits, and dandruff. There are also fact-filled pages on all of the body's systems and a link to a Teacher's Center with student activities.